W9-CCS-187

DISCARD

JUDE THE OBSCURE

A Paradise of Despair

Twayne's Masterwork Studies

Robert Lecker, General Editor

JUDE THE OBSCURE

A Paradise of Despair

Gary Adelman

Twayne Publishers • *New York*
Maxwell Macmillan Canada • *Toronto*
Maxwell Macmillan International • *New York Oxford Singapore Sydney*

823.8
Hardy

Twayne's Masterwork Studies No. 94

Jude the Obscure: A Paradise of Despair
Gary Adelman

Copyright © 1992 by Twayne Publishers
All rights reserved. No part of this book may be reproduced or transmitted in any
form or by any means, electronic or mechanical, including photocopying, recording,
or by any information storage and retrieval system, without permission in writing
from the Publisher.

Twayne Publishers   Maxwell Macmillan Canada, Inc.
Macmillan Publishing Company   1200 Eglinton Avenue East
866 Third Avenue   Suite 200
New York, New York 10022   Don Mills, Ontario M3C 3N1

Macmillan Publishing Company is part of the Maxwell Communication Group
of Companies.

Library of Congress Cataloging-in-Publication Data

Adelman, Gary.
    Jude the obscure : a paradise of despair / Gary Adelman.
        p.   cm. — (Twayne's masterwork studies ; no. 94)
    Includes bibliographical references and index.
    ISBN 0-8057-9435-2 (alk. paper) : $22.95. — ISBN 0-8057-8563-9
(alk. paper) : $7.95
    1. Hardy, Thomas, 1840–1928.   Jude the obscure.   2. Despair in
literature.   I. Title.   II. Series.
PR4746.A75   1992
823'.8—dc20   92-10829
                                                                       CIP

The paper used in this publication meets the minimum requirements of American
National Standard for Information Sciences—Permanence of Paper for Printed
Library Materials. ANSI Z3948-1984. ⊗ ™

10 9 8 7 6 5 4 3 2 1 (hc)
10 9 8 7 6 5 4 3 2 1 (pb)

Printed in the United States of America

SSB

For my mother and father

There is an electric fire in human nature tending to purify—so that among these human creatures there is continuously some birth of new heroism—the pity is that we must wonder at it; as we should at finding a pearl in rubbish.

—*John Keats*

A picture of my existence . . . would portray a useless stake covered with snow and frost, fixed loosely and slantwise into the ground in a deeply ploughed field on the edge of a great plain on a dark winter's night.

—*Franz Kafka*

CONTENTS

ILLUSTRATIONS

Note on the References and Acknowledgments

All page references to *Jude the Obscure* are to the Norton Critical Edition, edited by Norman Page (New York and London: W. W. Norton & Company, 1978). The first number cited parenthetically in the text refers to the part, followed by a colon and chapter number of the citation.

I wish to take this opportunity to thank Judith Liebman, and the Research Board of the University of Illinois, for supporting my work and making available the invaluable assistance of Michael Armstrong and Norma Marder, who edited the manuscript. I am especially indebted to Norma for the overall clarity and finish of the work. I am also indebted to Elsie Pettit and Anne Moore for their assistance. Lastly, I wish to thank my wife, Phyllis Rider Adelman, for finding time to carefully proof the manuscript and make final refinements. Copies of the Macbeth-Raeburn illustrations to the first edition of *Jude the Obscure* were obtained from the Dorset County Museum in Dorchester and are reprinted with their permission. The frontispiece was designed for this book by Carlton Bruett.

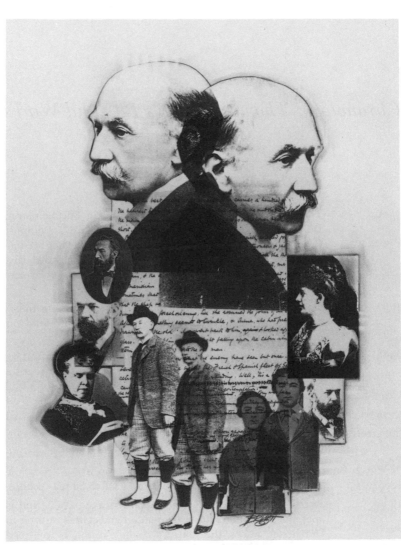

Frontispiece by Carlton Bruett

Chronology: Thomas Hardy's Life and Works

1840	Thomas Hardy is born, almost stillborn, in Bockhampton, Dorsetshire on 2 June. His father, Thomas Hardy, a violinist for the church choir, is a stonemason who would later become a prosperous master mason. His mother, Jemima Hand Hardy, maidservant and cook, is remarkably well-read; her favorite work is Dante's *Divine Comedy*.
1841	Hardy's sister Mary is born. Sharing his interests in music and literature, she would be his closest confidante until his marriage.
1848	Begins school in Lower Bockhampton. An obsessive affection develops between the boy and his teacher, pious Julia Augusta Martin. His mother gives him Dryden's translation of Virgil and Samuel Johnson's *Rasselas*.
1849	After transferring to a school in Dorchester, he begins to learn Latin. The separation from his teacher Mrs. Martin is traumatic for them both.
1850	Brother Henry is born.
1855	Hardy becomes a teacher at Stinsford Church Sunday school.
1856	Second sister Katherine is born. Hardy leaves school and is apprenticed to John Hicks, an architect and church restorer in Dorchester. Hicks, the son of a country rector, is well-read in ancient and modern literature. Hardy's fellow apprentice, Henry Bastow, has literary, scholarly, and religious interests. The three have lively intellectual discussions. Hardy continues to study Latin and begins Greek. Most of his studying is done from 5 AM to 8 AM, before work; after work he plays the violin for local dances and weddings.
1857	Meets Horatio Mosley (Horace) Moule, classical scholar and teacher, man of letters, published poet and critic, accomplished musician, and depressive alcoholic. Moule helps Hardy with his Greek, directs his reading, introduces him to the conflict

between orthodox Christianity and modern thought as well as to the liberal *Saturday Review*, encourages him to write, and provides the most intimate male friendship that Hardy will ever experience. Moule would later be one of the models for Jude.

1859   Charles Darwin publishes *On the Origin of Species*.

1860   Moule and Hardy discuss Darwin's work and *Essays and Reviews*, a volume by seven scholars that subjects the Bible to modern textual and interpretive criticism. At Oxford Thomas Henry Huxley and Bishop Samuel Wilberforce stormily debate on evolution vs. orthodoxy.

1861   Still orthodox, Hardy begins intensive study of the Bible, the Book of Common Prayer, and Keble's *Christian Year*.

1862   Hardy moves to London and works for Arthur Blomfield, architect and church restorer. He corresponds extensively with Moule and frequents the opera, the theaters, the International Exhibition, and the National Gallery. He is a fascinated observer of London's lower classes and especially its prostitutes, of whom there are some 80,000, many of them children. He immerses himself in the works of Huxley, J. S. Mill, and Herbert Spencer and begins moving toward agnosticism. Eventually he rejects the doctrines of providence, redemption, and immortality, but he would remain a lover of church services all his life. He reads Shelley intensively, heavily penciling his two-volume edition.

1863   The Royal Institute of British Architects awards Hardy a prize for his essay "On the Application of Colored Bricks and Terra Cotta to Modern Architecture," his first publication.

1866   An admirer of Algernon Charles Swinburne's *Atalanta in Calydon* and *Poems and Ballads*, Hardy is indignant about the attacks on the poet's pagan sensuality. Contemplates entering Cambridge with a view to serving the Church but abandons the plan on realizing that his funds, his training, and his faith are all insufficient. Writes the poem "Hap."

1867   Returns to Dorchester and works for church restorer John Hicks. Writes draft of the novel "The Poor Man and the Lady" (never published), which contains poems written during the London years. "Walks out" with his 16-year-old cousin Tryphena Sparks, a pupil-teacher. About this time he sees much of his uncle John Antell, by trade a shoemaker, a prodigy of self-education, having some competence in Latin, Greek, and even Hebrew. Frustrated ambition drives Antell to drink, bitterness, and an early grave. In an early draft of *Jude the Obscure*, "Jude" is called "Jack."

1869 Hardy's novel "The Poor Man and the Lady" is rejected by publishers Chapman and Hall, but their reader, George Meredith, encourages Hardy to write another novel.

1870 While inspecting a church restoration job in St. Juliot, Cornwall, Hardy falls in love with the rector's sister-in-law, Emma Lavinia Gifford.

1871 After much rewriting, Hardy publishes *Desperate Remedies* at his own expense. Critical response is mixed; one negative review makes him wish he were dead. Emma Gifford encourages him to continue writing.

1872 *Under the Greenwood Tree* published and favorably received. Begins *A Pair of Blue Eyes*. Emma Gifford's father violently objects to their engagement.

1873 Visits Horace Moule, now living in Cambridge. *Far from the Madding Crowd* begins serial publication in the *Cornhill Magazine*. In September Hardy is deeply shocked to hear that Moule has cut his throat with a razor. "H. H. M." and "my friend" recur in Hardy's poems for years to come.

1874 Marries Emma Gifford; the marriage producs no children.

1876–1878 *The Hand of Ethelberta* published (1876). Hardys reside at Sturminster Newton. Hardy later refers to this period of his marriage as an "idyll . . . our happiest time." Writes most of *The Return of the Native* (published 1878).

1880 *The Trumpet-Major* published. As he becomes increasingly famous, Hardy moves in literary circles and meets Robert Browning, Alfred, Lord Tennyson, and Edmund Gosse. Working on *A Laodicean* (published 1881), Hardy suffers an internal hemorrhage; confined to bed, he must dictate much of the novel to his wife.

1881 Hardy moves to Dorsetshire.

1882 *Two on a Tower* published.

1883 Publishes "The Dorsetshire Labourer," an article on economic exploitation of farm workers. Begins work on *The Mayor of Casterbridge*. Designs his own house, Max Gate (finished in 1885), outside Dorchester, but henceforth he spends several months of each year in London society.

1886 *The Mayor of Casterbridge* published. Hardy is now wearing a beard trimmed in the Elizabethan manner, which he will

	shave off in 1890, leaving only the moustache. He is a small man (five feet six inches), rather frail, balding, shy in manner, with a shrewd birdlike glance and a slightly hooked nose.
1887	*The Woodlanders* published.
1888	Conceives of a short story about a young man unable to go to Oxford, his subsequent struggles, and his ultimate suicide— probably the germ of *Jude the Obscure*. Publishes *Wessex Tales*, his first collection of short stories.
1890	Death of Hardy's cousin Tryphena Sparks. Hardy calls her his "lost prize" and uses his memories of her in creating Sue Bridehead.
1891	Emma Hardy begins a secret diary in which she records her objections to her husband's conduct and beliefs. Serial publication of *Tess of the d'Urbervilles* in bowdlerized form after several publishers have rejected it. Hardy publishes *A Group of Noble Dames* (short stories) and *Tess of the d'Urbervilles* (book form). Many reviews of *Tess* are favorable, but Hardy is angered by attacks on the novel's sexual morality and implied theology. Preparing to work on *Jude*, Hardy pays a visit to his sister Mary's teachers' training college at Salisbury, which will become the model for Sue Bridehead's teachers' college.
1892	Hardy's father dies, leaving an estate of £850 (equivalent to £20,000 in modern currency). Serial publication of *The Pursuit of the Well-Beloved* in October, November, and December. Begins work on *Jude the Obscure*. His wife's eccentricities are worsening and sometimes suggest mental aberration; over the next few years the couple become increasingly estranged.
1893	On a visit to Dublin, Hardy meets authoress Florence Henniker, "a charming intuitive woman," to whom he forms a one-sided attachment. Mrs. Henniker is the immediate inspiration for Sue Bridehead.
1894	From August to May Hardy temporarily resumes his profession as architect and stonemason and works on a church restoration job in West Knighton. *Life's Little Ironies* (short stories) published. In December *Harper's Magazine* begins serial publication of *Jude the Obscure* in severely bowdlerized form; the serial continues until November 1895.
1895	*Jude the Obscure* published in book form in November. Emma Hardy detests the novel, and the reviews are savage.
1896	Bewildered and indignant, Hardy reacts to the attacks of reviewers and his wife through the poems "In Tenebris." He

resolves to write no more fiction and to devote himself to poetry. In October he notes, "Perhaps I can express more fully in verse ideas and emotions which run counter to the inert crystallized opinion—hard as a rock—which the vast body of men have vested interest in supporting." His poetic oeuvre will eventually comprise nine hundred poems published in various collections until his death, the last appearing posthumously. Visits the field of Waterloo in preparation for writing *The Dynasts*. Works on prefaces and revisions for the Uniform Edition (1895–97) of all his novels, as he will later do again for the Wessex Edition (1912). Learns to ride and becomes an avid bicyclist.

1897 *The Well-Beloved* published in book form.

1898 *Wessex Poems*, his first volume of verse, published. The reviews are partly hostile, partly puzzled. Emma Hardy dislikes the poems.

1904 Death of Hardy's mother. Publishes part 1 of *The Dynasts*, an epic of Napoleonic times. Part 2 will be published in 1906, part 3 in 1908.

1905 Visits Swinburne; the two authors are amused at a newspaper's remark: "Swinburne planteth, Hardy watereth, and Satan giveth the increase."

1907 The Hardys are invited by King Edward VII to a garden party at Windsor Castle.

1909 Succeeds George Meredith as president of the Society of Authors.

1910 Awarded the Order of Merit; receives the keys to the city of Dorchester.

1912 Hardy receives the gold medal of the Royal Society of Literature. Shortly after a violent quarrel, Emma Hardy, who had been growing increasingly unstable, dies on 27 November.

1913 Hardy's grief and remorse inspire more than one hundred poems. He makes a pilgrimage to St. Juliot, where he had first met Emma. Receives honorary Litt. D. from Cambridge.

1914 At age 74 Hardy marries his secretary, Florence Dugdale, age 35. *Satires of Circumstance* (including "Poems of 1912–1913") published. The outbreak of World War I deepens his pessimism and strengthens his disbelief in any "ultimate wisdom at the back of things."

1917 Begins working with his wife Florence on his autobiography. In accordance with his wishes, she would publish it, after his death, as her own work: *The Early Years of Thomas Hardy 1840–1891* (1928); *The Later Years of Thomas Hardy 1892–1928* (1930).

1919   *Collected Poems* published.

1920   Awarded an honorary Litt. D. from Oxford (Jude's "Christminster").

1927   Undergraduates of Balliol College, Oxford (Jude's "Biblioll College"), perform Euripides' *Iphigeneia at Aulis* at Max Gate.

1928   Thomas Hardy dies at Max Gate on 11 January, leaving an estate worth 2 million pounds in modern currency. His ashes are buried in Westminster Abbey. At the same hour, Hardy's heart, which had been removed from his body, is buried in Emma Hardy's grave in Stinsford churchyard, Dorsetshire.

1930   *Collected Poems* (fourth edition) published posthumously.

Literary and Historical Context

1

Historical Context

Until he was 25, Hardy considered entering the Church of England. He attended Sunday service in the evening as well as in the morning, developed an early habit of applying biblical texts to his own life, and had so much the look of the fresh-faced Victorian parson that his family took it for granted that he would make a career of the Church. He knew by heart John Keble's pocket book of Christian verse, *The Christian Year*, which consisted of poems of orthodox sentiment designed for every Sunday and holy day, and the Brady and Tate metrical version of the Psalms, which was included in the back of the Book of Common Prayer.[1] In 1860 he studied Greek, using Griesbach's edition of the New Testament (like Jude), and was punctilious in his practice of orthodoxy with a view to preparing himself for Cambridge and the ministry. The typical parson had a university education and could read the Hebrew and Greek texts of the Bible. But the typical parson was also a gentleman, and it is doubtful whether as a stonemason's son and an assistant in a London architectural firm with a salary of £110 per year Hardy could have ever afforded Cambridge.

During medieval times, the majority of Oxford and Cambridge scholars were ecclesiastics; the Church needed a large supply of skilled clerics and therefore recruited a number of these scholars from among the poor. But gradually matriculants who were sons of clergymen and country gentlemen became more predominant. By the mid-eighteenth century, only an eighth of the Oxford entrants were plebeians, and of this class of farmers, small businessmen, and artists, the poor constituted an even smaller fraction. The university reforms of the mid-nineteenth century effectively disqualified the poor altogether. They abolished the system by which poor students earned the £135 for annual costs by acting as servants for the wealthy ones. Because the university entrance exams instituted by the reformers required expensive specialized training and private tutors, poor students could no longer compete. They were also greatly disadvantaged by the Greek requirement for entrance, although Greek was no longer taught in the grammar schools. Therefore Oxford, the Christminster of Jude's dreams, had never before been so socially exclusive as it was in the mid-nineteenth century when the plebeian population dropped to less than one-half of one percent.

Yet Hardy was less frustrated professionally by social conditions than was his shoemaker uncle, John Antell, who had achieved some competence in Greek and Hebrew and had learned enough Latin to open a school in Puddletown but could get no closer to his dream of a university education than could Jude Fawley. Hardy saw a good deal of Antell in the late 1860s after he had left London to work as an architect in his hometown. He would sit in his uncle's workroom at the back of the shop listening "to many tirades on the fundamental injustice of man's fate."[2]

By then the new scientific thought had destroyed Hardy's faith. He had abandoned the idea of Cambridge and the Church and was caught up in what was, in retrospect, a revolution in European cultural history. Darwin made it increasingly difficult for intellectuals to believe that man was a separate act of creation. When *On the Origin of Species* (1859) introduced the idea that chance begot order, for many contemporaries this idea wrecked the universe that existed in the imagination and that was depicted in countless stained-glass windows. The volume *Essays and Reviews*, which gained ready popularity in 1860, was the collaborative effort of Oxford professors who used scientific methods to attack conventional orthodoxy. It roused an especially virulent response because its authors were all clergymen of the Church of England. The most famous of them, Benjamin Jowett, Regius Professor of Greek, was prosecuted for heresy for contradicting a literal interpretation of the Bible, but the moral victory went to the accused. Thomas Henry Huxley and John Tyndall were especially effective advocates of the new thought; in particular, the tall, stern figure of Huxley made an indelible impression when he defended Darwin's theory at Oxford in 1860 against the ridicule of Bishop Wilberforce:

> "I asserted—and I repeat—that a man has no reason to be ashamed of having an ape for his grandfather. If there were an ancestor whom I should feel shame in recalling, it would rather be a man—a man of restless and versatile intellect—who, not content with an equivocal success in his own sphere of activity, plunges into scientific questions with which he has no real acquaintance, only to obscure them by an aimless rhetoric, and distract the attention of his hearers from the real point at issue by eloquent digressions and skilled appeals to religious prejudice."[3]

John Stuart Mill, and especially his treatise *On Liberty* (1862) with its compelling exhortations to think for oneself, exercised a great influence on Hardy.[4]

Many, Darwin among them, found that the open-endedness of evolution, the process by which human beings ascended from apes, inspired hope of a higher destiny and an impetus for good. But liberation from ignorance and superstition affected Hardy differently. Blind chance seemed to govern a universe in which minute accidental variations in the species accounted for the evolution of human beings. God had been displaced, or, worse, satanized. "Wo is me, that my sojourning is prolonged!" Hardy wrote inside the back cover of his copy of *The Missal for the Use of the Laity* (Millgate 1982, 411). All Hardy's tragic protagonists murmur a similar lament, Jude most bitterly. The deracinated heroes of his great tragic novels—Clym Yeobright, Angel Clare, Sue and Jude—suffer from rationalism; it is a flaw, or monomania, that stunts them emotionally. The revolutionary scientific thought of the nineteenth century, which destroyed Hardy's faith, would, he believed, gradually deaden everyone's zest for life. He presents little Father Time as the child of a future haunted by the insignificance of momentary life in the vast waste of geological time, an emblem of "the coming universal wish not to live."[5]

Although every instinct of Hardy's intelligence went out to greet the new scientific thought, he was restrained by a temperamental attachment to Christianity and a nostalgic longing for a rural England that was disappearing. David Cecil says that Hardy's pessimism "is of a kind only possible to one indissolubly wedded to Christian standards of value. Christian teachers have always said that there was no alternative to Christianity but pessimism, that if Christian doctrine was not true, life was a tragedy. Hardy quite agreed with them. But he could not think the doctrine true, all the same. He found it impossible to believe the Christian hope."[6]

■　　■　　■

The marriage question, women's rights, the idea that women like workingmen were victims of oppression (women because of sex rather than class) were very much in the air when Hardy was writing *Jude*. The feminists' mission to overthrow the double standard had become in the last twenty years of the nineteenth century almost a crusade. Female sexuality and the woman's role in marriage had become so much a matter of discussion that unself–conscious writing about these subjects was impossible.[7]

In 1890 Ireland's hope of independence died when Captain O'Shea brought a divorce action against his wife that named Charles Stuart Parnell, the Irish nationalist leader, as her lover. The controversy caused by the scandal continued to occupy the newspapers, becoming a cause célèbre. Between 1889 and 1896 English versions of Ibsen's controversial plays were first produced in London, and Hardy saw performances of *Hedda Gabler, Rosmersholm,* and *The Master Builder* and probably knew *A Doll's House* and *Ghosts.* Thus the social atmosphere of the late 1800s stimulated Hardy to explore in *Jude* the marriage question and especially (in Sue) the dilemmas of the woman's position in the social structure.

Until 1870, divorce was possible only by means of an act of Parliament. As late as 1890, only six hundred divorce cases went through the courts in a year. Women could not gain admission to legal or other professions, and they could not control property or protect themselves against their husbands' brutality. Prior to 1878 they were not entitled to separation and payment of maintenance if their husband was convicted for aggravated assault, and prior to 1886 they had no rights to maintenance if they were deserted. All physical, moral, and economic arguments were against the employment of women in the civil service and other professions. Those who had not the tutoring to become governesses became domestic servants, mine and factory workers, or prostitutes. Because one-twelfth of unmarried women in mid-Victorian England were prostitutes, prior to 1886 all working-class women were subject to compulsory inspection and treatment under the Contagious Diseases Act of the 1860s on the grounds that they were prostitutes.

Queen's College, the first college opened for women, was established in 1848 for the sole purpose of providing a proper education for governesses. Women were first allowed to take degrees at the University of London in 1880, and although women's colleges were established at Cambridge and Oxford in 1869 and 1879 respectively, women could not take degrees there until after World War I. Towards 1900, women began to be able to make their living in shops, offices, and in the civil service, as well as in teaching and nursing. They only received the right to vote in 1918 as a reward for their contribution to the war effort.

Yet Hardy's attack on society's sexual codes and customs, his interest in the "new woman," and particularly his attempts to idealize in Jude and Sue a love that is passionate without being sexual derive less from the polemic and debate of the 1890s than from his own peculiar personal history. He was a delicate child and developed an extreme emotional dependency on his mother, who became the driving force behind his continued self-improvement. When he was only eight years old, she gave him Johnson's *Rasselas* and a translation of the *Aeneid*. Hardy describes himself as "a child till he was sixteen, a youth till he was five-and-twenty, and a young man till he was nearly fifty" (Millgate 1982, 23). Both his biographers say that he developed sexually very late, if he developed at all, and that according to a family tradition he was sexually impotent (Gittings 1975, 29; Millgate 1982, 354). The tenacity of the maternal bond seems evident in Hardy's relationship to three of his cousins. All three cousins were daughters of his mother's sister and had the features of his mother. He made adolescent advances to Rebecca Sparks and later wished to marry both her sisters—Martha, who was six years older than Hardy, and Tryphena (later one of the models for Sue Bridehead). He later developed the pattern of speculating about almost every woman he met and of passing from one to another, sexually curious but without sexual involvement.

Hardy met his wife-to-be, Emma Gifford, in northern Cornwall, where he had gone to make plans for the restoration of an old church. She was a lady, the sister-in-law of the rector. They married in 1874 after a long courtship, and as the years passed they became miserable. After 1885 they lived at Max Gate, a nondescript and inhospitable house, very gloomy owing to the two to three thousand Austrian pines Hardy planted, possibly to enhance his moodiness. They tried to shut their eyes and ears to each other: Hardy stayed in his brown study or went away to London; Emma spent time in her attic study where she pursued her own literary ambitions and interested herself in church affairs. They maintained the rituals of marriage, bicycling, attending church, and taking meals together. This was the central tragedy of Hardy's life: his relationship with a woman whom he found vain and rather stupid, tiresomely jealous of his reputation, and dumpy and coarse-faced, a woman who gradually became unstable from resentment and loneliness, who protested against his self-containment, his artistic temperament, his flirtations with society women, and the irreligion and immorality of his books. Yet during the year following her death in 1912, the 72-year-old Hardy wrote more than one hundred love poems to his deceased Emma. Such was his muse. He fed on a ghostly sustenance, a personal despair possibly rooted in sexual impotence.

Millgate suspects that Hardy's mentor, Horace Moule, one of the chief models for Jude, was homosexual (1982, 156). Perhaps Hardy saw himself in his friend, saw an image of the tragedy of his own life, whichever way he turned, married or single. Moule was eight years older than Hardy, a member of Queen's College, Cambridge, and a superb teacher of classical history. Hardy was an emotionally immature yet strangely learned boy of 17 when they met in 1857 and he became Moule's pupil. Moule was physically as well as intellectually attractive, with a "sensitive, almost feminine face" (Gittings 1975, 41). Far more than a mere tutor, Moule provided a university of courses to the self-taught Hardy, and he was Hardy's counselor and friend as well. But there was a tragic side to Moule's life. He isolated himself from his family, he quit his teaching position at a boy's school, he had a drinking problem, and he fathered a bastard child who was brought up in Australia and was hanged there; and this illegitimate child was probably the germ of little Father Time. In 1873 Horace Moule cut his throat with a razor.

The shock of Moule's suicide was momentous; Hardy may have seen in Moule his dark twin and may have subsequently sought through his fiction to control his own suicidal wish. Gittings says that from the time of Moule's death "the tragic and defeated hero arrives for good in all Hardy's works," that thereafter "Hardy never portrayed a man who was not, in some way, maimed by fate," and that "we can date the emergence of Hardy as a fully tragic artist, and expounder of man's true miseries, from the suicide of his friend" (Gittings 1975, 183; 186).

2

The Importance of the Work

Jude is the last of the fourteen novels Hardy wrote between the ages of 30 and 55, most of them about the countryside and country people of Dorset, where he lived most of his life. His books reflect the changes the region was undergoing as well as the ideological contradictions of the late nineteenth century. Social innovation made Hardy uneasy: by the time he wrote *Jude* he questioned all social conventions—the sanctity of the marriage contract as well as faith in progress and modernity.

Jude is about the tension of being caught between two historical worlds, and it reflects Hardy's ambivalence about the dilemmas of his time more powerfully than anything else he wrote. The book was subversive in its time. It affronted accepted moral standards chiefly because it sympathetically portrays a hero and heroine who live together and have children out of wedlock. Hardy had the daring to declare that marriage is usually unhappy, and furthermore he blamed society, in part, for the tragic consequences of Jude and Sue's love—as if their tragedy was a form of oppression, as if they were victims rather than sinners.

The idea that Hardy is struggling to create a subversive art in *Jude* is an attractive theory: his book has an unnerving effect, because, whatever his intentions might have been, the novel is intimately concerned with class and sex oppression—with a rapidly changing society, with the effects of different levels of education on the community, and with a search for a form of life tolerable to an intelligent, sensitive woman.

Yet Hardy was at the same time uneasy about displacing the old codes of life, and while he raises philosophical and religious questions and is concerned with the problems of class and social mobility, as well as with the question of a woman's place in society, he undermines Jude and Sue, subverting his novel's heterodoxy by constantly shifting the point of view from high seriousness to satire and farce. In addition, most of the epigraphs to each of the parts of the novel imply criticism and even mockery of Jude and Sue. From one perspective they are the victims of sexual and economic exploitation; from another, they are victims of their own folly.

But there is also a larger view, a poetic vision of overwhelming destiny, of tragedy, from which perspective Jude is doomed from the first. Hardy's metaphysical pessimism articulates a world in which individuals are the playthings of malevolent or indifferent forces that destroy their happiness, beating them down and making a mockery of their lives. The tragic view behind the social drama has different effects on different readers: to some it confers a deep and solemn beauty upon the story, to others a Schopenhauerian gloom and sense of futility. This near and far vision—a foreground of crossing perspectives in which there is no overriding point of view and the hero is alternately thwarted by society and by his own folly; and a background, or worldview, that mocks endeavor and portrays the existential absurdity of life—is one of the remarkable features of Hardy's last novel. Such artistry enables Hardy to have it both ways: he mocks Jude for his simplicity yet praises his high-mindedness; he satirizes Jude's predicament yet bitterly indicts the obstructive prejudice of his society—all the while lowering upon the scene a sardonic forecast of disaster. Hardy's is the method of an ironist par excellence.

The heart of the novel is a love story that fascinates the reader although there is something repellent about it. Possibly Sue is the most successful representation in Victorian literature of the dilemmas of women trying to escape their victimization. Nevertheless, our admiration for her is far from unequivocal. She is a woman who loves to be loved but does not like sex—a coquette who treats her captive lovers with astounding cruelty. In the end she breaks Jude's heart, and the secret power of the novel lies in the way Hardy refuses to allow us to judge her and makes us participate in something equivalent to Jude's neurotic compulsion to love her. The novel is a masterpiece in the art of reader seduction, a story of transcendent and ennobling, debilitating and shameful love.

Hardy was regarded as the greatest living English novelist during his lifetime, a reputation based on his power to create sensuous illusions of people and physical settings, to relate a tragic story of passion and make the settings its metaphor, and to enchant the scene with an extraordinary character, usually a woman. *Jude* is the most ambitious and complex of his novels: it is remarkable for its haunting pathos, complexity of narrative voice and perspective, characterization of Sue, and for its sense of intimate disclosure, of our being present with the private man in his paradise of despair.

3

Critical Reception

EARLY CRITICISM

Only one note relevant to *Jude* appears in Hardy's ghosted autobiography: April 1888: "A short story of a young man—'who could not go to Oxford'—His struggles and ultimate failure. Suicide. There is something the world ought to be shown, and I am the one to show it to them."[1] According to the preface to the first edition of *Jude*, the idea for the novel "was jotted down in 1890, from notes made in 1887 and onwards."[2]

Hardy's creative output was remarkable during the six years or so between the inception of *Jude* and its appearance as a serial in *Harper's Magazine*. He wrote and published *Tess of the d'Urbervilles* and *The Well-Beloved*, and he issued two collections of short stories, *A Group of Noble Dames* and *Life's Little Ironies*. *Jude* appeared first in an emasculated form[3] in *Harper's* under the title "The Simpletons;" then the title was changed to "Hearts Insurgent" after the first installment; finally the novel was published in book form in November 1895 as *Jude the Obscure*. Shortly after the publication Hardy wrote the three parts of "In Tenebris" and "Wessex Heights"—four of the most powerful and bleakly spare of his poems—and the reviews of *Jude the Obscure* may have helped to inspire them.

The reviews of *Tess of the d'Urbervilles* had been on the whole sensitively appreciative; yet Hardy was very thin-skinned regarding criticism. "[I]f this sort of thing continues," he noted in reply to a nasty review of *Tess*, "no more novel-writing for me. A man must be a fool to deliberately stand up to be shot at" (Millgate 1982, 321). Although *Jude* was also appreciated, the negative reaction to it was so startlingly abusive that one may well believe his grim remark years later (in the preface to the 1912 edition) that the critical reception completely cured him of further interest in novel writing. He was attacked for exhibiting his Zolaesque taste for the coarsely indecent, for "trailing his talents in the dirt," for having written a book "steeped in sex." One reviewer called it "Jude the Obscene"; a bishop claimed he had burned the novel in disgust; a New York reviewer said she ran to the window for air after reading *Jude*; and Hardy received a box of ashes, presumably those of his novel, from one of his irate readers.

Mrs. Oliphant, writing for the conservative *Blackwood's Magazine*, was so outraged by *Jude* that she came close to sputtering expletives. "There may be books more disgusting," she said, "more impious as regards human nature, more foul in detail, in those dark corners where the amateurs of filth find garbage to their taste."[4] Although she had written with laudatory appreciativeness of *Tess*, *Jude* so offended her that she tried with every stroke of her pen to draw blood. Referring to Hardy's depiction of Arabella and her girlfriends handling the privates of a pig, Oliphant wrote, "[T]he country lasses at their outdoor work [are] more brutal in depravity than anything which the darkest slums could bring forth" (Cox, 259).

Edmund Gosse had a problem in reviewing the novel for *Cosmopolis* because he was Hardy's friend but disliked *Jude*. The general point of his review is that the book would have been "stronger, and even more tragic, if Mr. Hardy did not appear in it as an advocate taking sides with his unhappy hero" (Cox, 267). The novel strikes him as too artificial; the composition is too symmetrical; and the whole book is a manipulation in the service of an idea. Although cautious not to hurt the feelings of his thin-skinned friend, Gosse concludes quite cuttingly,

"We wish [Hardy] would go back to Egdon Heath and listen to the singing in the heather [that is, return to writing books in which nature is a powerful presence, and there is no social criticism]. And as to the conversations of his semi-educated characters [a dig at the self-taught Hardy], they are really terrible. Sue and Jude talk a sort of University Extension jargon that breaks the heart" (Cox, 269).

The early and later reviewers share an objection to little Father Time and his murders and suicide; namely, that the murders break, or nearly break, the spell, turning tragedy into ghastly farce. "We all know perfectly well that baby Schopenhauers are not coming into the world in shoals," declares the unsigned reviewer of the *Illustrated London News*, who writes fretfully about the novel—full of admiration for Hardy yet troubled by the discomforting feeling of being hoodwinked. "The perpetual shuffling of partners hovers dangerously near the ridiculous," he exclaims; notwithstanding, he concludes, "read the story how you will, it is manifestly a work of genius" (Cox, 275–76).

Among the laudatory reviews, Havelock Ellis's (in the *Savoy Magazine*) has the distinction of attempting to account for the negative reaction to what he considers a literary masterpiece. One point in his review that is especially worth noting is that Hardy is in love with the instinctive world of nature, with all that is uncontrolled by artificial constraint, and that this love of the primitive and unfettered makes him the loving student of women. Passionate love, particularly a woman in love, disregards all but "essential law," and therefore tragic love stories necessarily draw power from the conflict between the erotic impulse and society—from, on the one side, the "moral order in Nature," on the other, "the laws framed merely as social expedients without a basis in the heart of things, and merely expressing the triumph of the majority over the individual" (Cox, 310). Hardy's sensuousness as an artist shows that he is not much in sympathy with society, and sensuousness, combined with outspoken criticism, is his sin against societal law. Mrs. Oliphant let sensuousness pass as artistic beauty in *Tess*, but she felt defied, perhaps betrayed, by Hardy's outspoken heterodoxy and his identification with his "sinners" in *Jude*.

In 1914 D. H. Lawrence wrote his *Study of Thomas Hardy*—in

part a confession of the heart and a working out of the symbolic meaning of his novel, *The Rainbow* (1915), but most notably a classic interpretation of Hardy's novels. All literature, in Lawrence's view, is about coming into being or failing to come into being. In his literary criticism he always focuses on the repressive influence of culture, analyzing and bringing to light the unconscious predilections that sidetrack the artist's intention to celebrate freedom and a more abundant life. In the first part of the study, he shows that the pioneering characters that interest Hardy lack the necessary strength to bear isolation and exposure. These characters sidetrack themselves by either giving in to society or being destroyed by it—because Hardy despite himself must stand with the community against the individual interest. An inbred moral antagonism clogs his sympathy for those of his characters who make the break for freedom. In the second part of the study, Lawrence analyzes the source of this moral antagonism and suggests that Hardy's novels are allegories of Christianity's suppression of the erotic impulse. Christianity is in conflict with the new science and modernity; it is leagued with the rural life Hardy loved and saw crumbling all about him, the victim of industrialism. But these conflicts are chimeras, Lawrence argues. The real issue of the novels is failed liberation into adult sexuality; freedom is caught in the stranglehold of narcissistic and incestuous fantasies.[5]

PESSIMISM IN *JUDE*

Hardy criticism until the 1970s was inordinately concerned with the issue of pessimism. The critics' more general charge has been that Hardy subjects his characters to the action of the plot. According to E. M. Forster, the plot of a novel should not be an external necessity to which the characters are ordered to acquiesce; the plot should be a living expression of character—and not, as in Hardy, a contrivance or a "superb and terrible machine" for piling up agony.[6] Many critics agree with Forster that Hardy emphasizes causality more than his medium permits; but Virginia Woolf argues that those novels in which heroes battle against the decrees of fate do not deserve such criticism. To her, *The Mayor of Casterbridge* is sublime because Henchard is "pitted, not against another man, but against something outside himself which is opposed to men of his ambition and power."[7] Jude, by contrast, "carries on his miserable contest against the deans of colleges and the conventions of sophisticated society." He battles against the laws of men rather than the decrees of fate, and when the battle is against men, argument is allowed to dominate impression, and the author's explanations mar the effect and seem trivial (Woolf, 255). William Rutland agrees entirely with Woolf, deeming *Jude* "a treatise on the misery of human existence" and Jude himself "a puppet constructed for a didactic purpose, who is jerked by Hardy from the wings."[8]

D. H. Lawrence sees in the fatal machinery of Hardy's plots a fatal division in Hardy himself that expresses itself as a moral antagonism for the characters he loves, namely, those who attempt to live for themselves, free of the old, communal morality. "Therefore," according to Lawrence, "[Hardy] will create a more or less blameless individual and, making him seek his own fulfilment, his highest aim, will show him destroyed by the community, or by that in himself which represents the community, or by some close embodiment of the civic idea. Hence the pessimism. To do this, however, he must select his individual with a definite weakness, a certain coldness of temper, inelastic, a certain inevitable and inconquerable adhesion to the community. This is obvious in Troy, Clym, Tess, and Jude," and especially Sue (*Phoenix*, 439).[9]

More recently critics have explained Hardy's pessimism as the result of attempting to adapt Shelley's love fantasies in "The Revolt of Islam" and "Epipsychidion" to the realistic novel. Phyllis Bartlett, for instance, sees Sue "as Hardy's full-length, mature study of the Shelleyan woman . . . as he imagined she would disintegrate under the stress of child-bearing, poverty and social custom" and Jude's story as the "tragedy of a man captivated by so visionary a creature."[10]

Both Hardy's biographers emphasize the importance of Shelley's influence and stress that as a young man Hardy was never without his volume of Shelley. Critics have also frequently mentioned a temperamental similarity between Hardy and Schopenhauer. For example, William Rutland quotes the following paragraph from *The World as Will and Idea*, claiming that it "might, indeed, be the text upon which Jude is a sermon":

> [T]he great majority of men . . . are like clockwork, which is wound up, and goes it knows not why; and every time a man is begotten and born, the clock of human life is wound up anew to repeat the same old piece it has played innumerable times before, passage after passage, measure after measure, with insignificant variations. . . . And yet, and here lies the serious side of life, every one of these fleeting forms, these empty fancies, must be paid for by the whole will to live, in all its activity, with many and deep sufferings and finally with a bitter death. (Rutland, 98)

In the preface to the 1912 edition of *Jude*, Hardy has two things to say apropos of the charge of pessimism brought against him: first, "that there is a higher characteristic of philosophy than pessimism . . . which is truth. Existence is either ordered in a certain way, or it is not so ordered"; and second, "[d]iffering natures find their tongue in the presence of differing spectacles. Some natures become vocal at tragedy, some are made vocal by comedy, and it seems to me that to whichever of these aspects of life a writer's instinct for expression the more readily responds, to that he should allow it to respond" (*Personal Writings*, 49).

Point of View

The notion that Hardy's novel writing is a kind of ballad making is true for novels such as *Tess* and *The Return of the Native* in which "the coloring of imagination" that irradiates the incidents and situations is taken from the world of nature. They are novels about love and betrayal, but they are equally about the causes that excite passion— "with the operations of the elements, and the appearances of the visible universe; with storm and sunshine, with the revolutions of the seasons, with cold and heat."[11] This is not the case with *Jude* because the external world plays comparatively little part in its imaginative coloring. At times the novel seems to be about Hardy's ambivalence toward the story he is relating.

Hardy sees Jude in two lights, in essence expressing two attitudes simultaneously, portraying both a noble Jude and a weak Jude: a Jude he identifies with the figure of Christ, frames in delicate sacramental imagery, and loves passionately; and a Jude who is scoffed at, whose imagination is stocked with illusions, and who is shown in the cold light of parody.

Carl Weber and Lance St. John Butler see only the heroic Jude. Weber says that *Jude* is Hardy's *King Lear*, stripped of any adornment: "no room now for amusing rustics; no idyllic descriptions of apple orchards or poetic accounts of the seasons . . . no pretence, in short, that the worthy receive any other reward than that which Shakespeare's Cordelia shared with Goneril and Regan."[12]

Butler is stirred by the range and depth of Jude's eloquence and the passionate endurance of his defenseless, transient efforts. To Butler, the tragedy is not brutally pessimistic. Jude is a Prometheus-Christ figure who struggles to extricate himself from the labyrinth of nineteenth-century thought and courageously opens the door to a new millennium. In the end, "Jude's body is one more obscure corpse among the many scattered about that doorway: Hardy mourns over it, but the doors are not shut again."[13]

Philip Weinstein sees only the weak Jude. All along, he says, Jude's mind has been "permanently astray from, immune to, the sordid physical situations in which he finds himself."[14] At the end Jude lives within "the schizoid space between failed expectation and ignored actuality" (Weinstein, 134).

Ramon Saldivar claims that because Hardy does not enable the reader to choose one point of view or another, the novel is "an allegory of the breakdown of the referential system."[15] The result of Hardy's shifting point of view is that there is no "ideally sanctioned stable truth," and therefore *Jude* can only be described in compositional terms. To Saldivar, *Jude* is a pattern of reversals (Saldivar, 116–17).

But the truth is that any great and lasting work is ambiguous.

Vincent Newey provides an eloquent understanding of the novel's texture. Its ambiguity, he says, reflects the existential predicament of a man bound to illusory aims but kept alive by his aspirations. Jude's life is "a futile gesture, altering nothing," but at the same time it represents "a defiant resilience": "He may with equal force be thought a 'fool' for following a 'freak of his fancy,' . . . or one who nobly tried to 'reshape his course' according to his 'aptness or bent.' He may be a victim of social formulas . . . or of the spirit of the times, or of his own 'impulses—affections—vices.' . . . He may be an object of 'pity' or a subject for 'ridicule';. . . a truth-teller or an actor playing a part for the benefit of the mob."[16] According to Newey, Jude's aliveness is his inexhaustible vulnerability, and his suicide is probably the only moral position possible in a world in which there is no inviolable framework of belief and conduct, and it is a triumph of self-affirmation wrestling "boldly in the jaws of denial" (Newey, 39).

THE FORM OF *JUDE*

Critics have described the novel's structure in various ways: it has been likened to a sonata, or a series of downward steps, or a treadmill, or a series of tableaux vivants.

Norman Page says that the novel is constructed on serial patterns of blindness and vision. Jude has great powers of discernment but his sex urge and youthful dream of Christminster "unite in inducing a disastrous blindness to truth and reality."[17] Jude's idealistic notion of Christminster temporarily blinds him and he enters the city absorbed in his dream, as remote to its reality as a ghost. Later, standing within the heart of the city he has a vision of its true nature and wakes from his dream. He undergoes parallel experiences when falling in love with both Arabella and Sue.

Millgate suggests that the novel's highly self-conscious patterning of repeated delays in the steadily downward curve of the tragedy, the alternating doubt, fear, and hope, conveys a sense of the hollowness of existence and is modelled on Sophocles' *Oedipus*.[18]

J. I. M. Stewart says that there is a "formal obtrusiveness" in the manner in which Jude and Sue exchange positions—time and circumstances enlarging his views and narrowing hers—and that the plotting of this crossing pattern—Jude's progress to a loss of faith and Sue's to a "morbid religiosity"—constitutes the novel's design.[19]

According to Lance St. John Butler, *Jude* is a geometrical structure based on the four characters who are continuously being thwarted and driven back to zero: "Jude's profession never rises above that of stonemason—he is always thrust back to that. His last wife is his first wife, his deathbed is in the city of his earliest dreams, he dies childless as he was at the beginning of the novel, he is neglected at the end as he was at the beginning" (Butler 1978, 127). Sue is brought back to square one, because she is involved at the end in the same high-church Anglicanism as she was when Jude had first encountered her, and she is married again to her first husband. Phillotson is back to teaching school in Marygreen where he began.

A. Alvarez sees the novel as a series of tableaux vivants through which the lonely character Jude moves, the other characters existing only to illuminate aspects of his loneliness: "In one sense, the entire novel is simply the image of Jude magnified and subtly lit from different angles until he and his shadows occupy the whole Wessex landscape."[20] The other characters are represented as projections of Jude rather than as complete in themselves—existing only in relation to him. The two women and Phillotson symbolize Jude's hopeless and debilitating search for fulfillment: Sue represents the vanity of his intellectual life; Arabella, his lust for degradation; and Phillotson, as "a kind of Jude Senior," represents resignation to mediocrity.

Hardy speaks specifically of the form of the novel in two letters to Edmund Gosse on November 10 and 20, 1895. He says that the design of the book is a pattern of contrasts: "Sue & her heathen gods set against Jude's reading the Greek Testt; Christminster academical, Chr in the slums; Jude the saint, Jude the sinner . . . marriage, no marriage; & c. & c."[21] As for the plot device, Hardy explains, "The 'grimy' features of the story go to show the contrast between the ideal life a man wished to lead, & the squalid real life he was fated to lead.

The throwing of the pizzle, at the supreme moment of his young dream, is to sharply initiate this contrast" (*Letters* 2, 93).

A MARXIST READING

Peter Widdowson contends that Hardy is actually a social historian and reads *Jude* as a novel about the problematic relations between classes in a rapidly changing society. The spread of industrialism into Dorset, the tensions of interclass relations, sexual and economic exploitation, and the effect of different levels of education on the community: this is what constitutes "the fundamental texture of Hardy's fictional world."[22] Widdowson considers Hardy's "ghosted" autobiography (the biography Hardy wrote and assembled with the help of his second wife) a key to understanding class struggle in Hardy's fiction.

Widdowson maintains that Hardy had a "many-layered and schizophrenic" obsession with class and status that reflected his scrupulous efforts to conceal his lower-class origins—his connection to laborers and servants (Widdowson, 147). His mother, Jemima, was one of seven pauper children brought up on parish relief, and most of his maternal aunts and uncles (bricklayers, for the most part) remained in Puddletown. Yet after *Far from the Madding Crowd* (1874), and thanks to Leslie Stephen, Hardy was introduced into the upper class, which became his dominant social milieu. After moving into his Victorian mansion, Max Gate, in 1885, he did not mix with his people but visited with the gentry. Gittings, for instance, describes him bicycling into nearby Puddletown in the early 1890s resolutely ignoring his numerous relatives (Gittings 1975, 213). This need to carefully disguise his social origins, Widdowson argues, made Hardy acutely sensitive to the issue of class, especially the problems of relationships between those who are déclassé, like Jude and Sue. Most of Hardy's novels are concerned with the problems of upward mobility and reflect his confusion about class allegiance; but particularly in *Jude*, "his . . . most outspoken fiction" (Widdowson, 148), ambivalence is swamped by hostility to the exploitation, dispossession, and destructive illusions of a class society.

Widdowson says that Hardy's deeply alienated consciousness led him to believe that people do not control their own destinies; what controls them "is a class system which reproduces the dynamics of social and economic power in an 'absurd,' arbitrary, and divisive way" (Widdowson, 213–14). Jude and Sue are destroyed by fate, but they are also victimized by social and sexual repression, and the victimization "is not by any means presented as 'metaphysical,' but rather as a concrete, material, social process" (Widdowson, 74). Gloom and pessimism in Hardy's novels derive from his bitterly deterministic view that individuals are "ideologically and socially determined, 'circumstanced' by the subject-positions they occupy" (Widdowson, 213).

Nevertheless, according to Widdowson, Hardy is not generally perceived as a social commentator; rather, a mythologized Hardy has been created "to neutralize the class divisions of a capitalist society" (Widdowson, 71). This is a pastoral-English Thomas Hardy—the master of description and metaphorical use of nature, the elegist of the passing agricultural community, the tragedian of the universal struggle between men and fate—the Hardy to whom we turn for a quietist retreat from an overly civilized urban culture: the Hardy cast by "*passé belles-lettrism*" to express the "defeatist humanist values of the critic" (Widdowson, 25; 31).

A FEMINIST READING

Jude has been described as the "most feminist of all Victorian novels."[23] Sue may well be the most interesting of Hardy's female characters. She has been endlessly analyzed, most recently by feminists who interpret the novel as a tragedy in which Sue is the central figure, not Jude. To feminists, the pathos does not lie in a heroic view of Jude; instead the tragedy derives from Sue's failure to live as a sexual being.

In his early review of the novel, Gosse called Sue a frigid "degenerate" with a "poor extravagant brain," and "a terrible study in pathology" (Cox, 269). Hardy replied in a personal letter (20 November, 1895) that "there is nothing perverted or depraved in Sue's nature," that she is "painfully alert," and that her sexual instincts are healthy, "but unusually weak & fastidious" (*Letters* 2, 99). He added that Jude's inability to have her as freely as he desired helps to break his heart and that Sue is a type that has always attracted him.

Eleven years later, replying to the Fawcett Society's request for his support of the suffragist movement, Hardy wrote, "I have for a long time been in favour of woman-suffrage. I fear I shall spoil the effect of this information (if it has any) in my next sentence by giving you my reasons. I am in favour of it because I think the tendency of the woman's vote will be to break up the present pernicious conventions in respect of manners, customs, religion, illegitimacy, the stereotyped household (that it must be the unit of society), the father of a woman's child (that it is anybody's business but the woman's own), . . . & other matters which I got into hot water for touching on many years ago" (*Letters* 3, 238). Hardy sounds like a radical feminist who expects the Fawcett Society to find his views too extreme, probably because Millicent Garrett Fawcett was the spokeswoman for liberal feminists who at that time idealized marriage.

Hardy's assertion that he got into "hot water" by expressing radical views in *Jude the Obscure* supports Rosemarie Morgan's contention that *Jude* is concerned with the harsh Victorian codes that suppressed people, especially women, who were struggling to be independent in choosing their own way of life. Morgan believes that Sue is psychically impaired as a result of the repression enforced by society and the men in her life, whom she pleases by adopting male-approved female roles. Sue slips into an appealing little girl role, and then assumes an "ennobled role when her emotional anxieties are appeased. . . . Both submissive little-girl and saintly idol fulfil the function of being objects of approval whilst providing Sue with a shield against her other subjective self, which fears constant rejection or disapproval."[24]

Despite these psychological handicaps, Sue makes a determined effort to free herself from dependency and coercion. But the forces against her are overwhelming: she is thwarted not only by patriarchal mores but also by her father and by Jude. Sue's father, Morgan points out, rejected her mother and rejected her, so Sue's fear of her own sexuality originated in infancy when she incorporated her father's hatred of her mother into her own personality. Thus Morgan argues that Sue's return to Phillotson is a returning to the punitive father; it is "physically, sexually and emotionally a passage back to childhood, a way back to the self-image created in infancy. . . . which in its infantile sexlessness and hatred of its femaleness had won the hearts of those standing in judgement upon her" (Morgan, 132).

Morgan says that the mild and forbearing Jude "unwittingly enforces her subjugation" by ignoring her sexual reality. We get a glimpse of a sexually aroused Sue at the flower pavilion, where Jude represses her desire by never responding to her physical excitement with "a soft kiss, a warm embrace." As a result, Sue unconsciously recognizes his need for "a cool intellectual response" (Morgan, 151). Jude, in turn, cannot help molding the woman he loves according to the chaste, Victorian ideal. He is in love with an imaginary woman whom he has substituted for his ardent, hopeless dream of Christminster.

The Sue that Morgan perceives is "a vulnerable but self-camouflaging woman harbouring smothered or latent passions under a composed exterior . . . still sexually unawakened, not yet orgasmic" (Morgan, 148). She is deprived of "[t]he power to act at the deepest level of intimate sexual engagement," and this deprivation "becomes, in turn, a denial of full participation in sexual union, a denial of caring and sharing, and, ultimately, a denial of sexual equality" (Morgan, 154). To Morgan, the novel traces the tragic repercussions of this denial.

A Reading

4

A Reading of the Text

God must not engage in theology; the writer must not destroy by human reasonings the faith that art requires of us.

Jorge Luis Borges, Labyrinths

What does Cervantes' great novel mean? Much has been written on the question. Some see in it a rationalist critique of Don Quixote's hazy idealism. Others see it as a celebration of that same idealism. Both interpretations are mistaken because they both seek at the novel's core not an inquiry but a moral position.

Milan Kundera, The Art of the Novel

INTRODUCTION

The epigraphs to *Jude* are like gargoyles that grin ironically at Jude—at his dreams, at his work that has come to nothing, at the vanity of his unfulfilled aims. The quotations from Browning and Swinburne mock Jude's despair and death as romantic folly. The lines from Marcus Aurelius Antoninus blame Jude's and Sue's misfortunes on their mishandling of life, their defiance of society. On the other hand, the epigraph to the whole novel ("the letter killeth") argues just the opposite—that society should have accepted them as free spirits.

Picture a young man with sensitive features sitting against the wall of a pigsty, lost in reverie. The New Testament in Greek lies open on his lap. A splendid visionary city occupies his fancy, a place where men made perfect by learning have come to study. Imagine also a young woman, an ethereal being with shining features. She smiles at him in his reverie, a tender smile; she seems a softened and sweetened version of himself, as if they were twins. The idea of dwelling among the learned in the splendid city and loving this beautiful being inspires him, for although he is an orphan and has only the most elementary schooling, he has taught himself Greek and Latin. He is a stonemason who quotes from ancient books and reads exegetical scholarship with the dream of being ordained.

But now substitute for the visionary city the quadrangles of a university that is closed to all but the sons of the wealthy. Imagine its scholars complacently absorbed in irrelevance and superstition. In place of the seraphic young woman is the pretty married cousin of the sensitive young man; she admires herself for her ennobling influence but dislikes physical expressions of love.

The artist stands in a figurative sense before the large canvas of his work considering its contradictions. The initial problem is one of point of view. What perspective should he take? What tone of voice should he use? Is it to be a story of enlightenment, a tragicomic un- blinding and coming to maturity? But what constitutes maturity? Ac- quiescence to social convention? Defiance? And how should he deal with Jude's quite ordinary human desires? Should an encounter with a down-to-earth woman dispel his illusions, or should it degrade him by deflecting him from his sense of purpose? How should the "freezing negatives" such a hero suffers from every quarter influence the tone? Should the author express indignation, farce, or black comedy? What would be the effect of interjections in the author's voice?

Hardy responded to these problems with an ambiguous narrative point of view that is the chief marvel of the novel. During Jude's courtship of Arabella, for instance, the presentation is farce counter- pointed by acerbic authorial intrusions, but the satirical sting is aimed at the ordinances of marriage and social convention rather than at the hero. Here the line between sympathy and ridicule is very fine indeed; and this fine line disappears altogether in the novel's central relation- ship: the love between Jude and Sue. From a courtly perspective, Jude and Sue come as close as human beings can to the transcendent, spiritual ideal of love as elevation, striving. From a clinical perspective, only an eccentric temperament would value transcendent love; there appears to be something wrong with Jude, some clog or monomania, for he loves a woman who finds the sexual embrace degrading. At times the story is a grisly joke about a man condemned to love a spirit figure who is unfit for life in the real world. Jude's compliance and delight in Sue's bizarre treatment of him during her engagement to Phillotson and his elopement night with her in Aldbrickham, where their love-making consists of a recital of lines from Shelley's "Epipsychidion," were probably written in a mood of bitterness, and they have a farcical effect. But Hardy also believes in the ennobling influence of this love; the transcendent ideal receives a high-serious treatment from him, and Jude achieves stature on account of it.

Borges says, "God must not engage in theology; the writer must not destroy by human reasonings the faith that art requires of us."[1] In other words, the miracle and mystery that give a work of art its authority would be destroyed by a single, overriding point of view. Novels are inquiries; they do not state moral positions. What then does this novel mean? It is not a criticism of hazy idealism: Jude is not merely the ridiculous victim of impulses and affections. Nor is it a celebration of idealism: Jude is not the noble, failed architect of his destiny.

Some think that the novel's shifting point of view reflects the conflict between Hardy's social conditioning and his striving to create a revolutionary art. According to this argument, *Jude*, like *Anna Karenina*, is the poetic mirror of an epoch, revealing the artist's reactionary prejudices, and, more importantly, portraying the ideological struggle of the working class. Thus, when Hardy suggests that Jude and Sue are victims of social unrest, or that they are solely responsible for their misfortunes, this is construed as an imperfection in Hardy's thinking, the artist's failure to transcend the cultural prejudices of his time.

But one can also argue that Hardy is not interested in changing anything. Maybe he fears a future free of family men and churchgoers while he attacks the institution of marriage and the narrow letter of Christianity—his heterodoxy, in other words, cutting from past to future. Perhaps the blighting effect of his nihilism is to make his lovers immune from moral judgment. Certainly the complexity of voice and perspective neutralizes our ability to judge Jude and his illusions, and particularly his love for Sue; this complexity is the author's conscious effort to conceal the shame attached to an intimate fantasy. Jude, as Millgate suggests (1982, 350), is an ill-omened name—similar to Judas Iscariot and possibly connected to the idea of the Wandering Jew, both of which are associated with perpetual homelessness and pariahdom. Hardy wrote the powerful first-person "In Tenebris" poems and "Wessex Heights" during the same year, 1896, when *Jude* was published, and all four poems are about pariahdom: they depict a sense of isolation, the despair of loneliness coupled with the longing for solitude. Hardy gave up novel writing after *Jude* and wrote poetry for the next 32 years, perhaps because the private man had revealed too much of himself in his novels. Poetry was safer than a realistic novel, for in a lyrical poem he did not have to dramatize the consequence of his own fantasies in terms of actual human life.

It seems to me altogether appropriate that a novel that is so much about shame should disguise its purposes so well. Jude is ashamed of being an unwanted orphan, and of his degrading marriage. He is ashamed of having attempted to drown himself like his mother did, and of loving his cousin. He is ashamed of wasting his studies, and of having deluded himself about the priesthood. He is ashamed of having become a half-educated jack-of-all-trades. Sue, for that matter, is ashamed of being an unwanted child, of being unloved by her father, of manipulating men, and of her thoughts, fantasies, and unconventional behavior. She lives with one eye looking back over her shoulder fearful of retributive consequences.

Yet Hardy refuses to allow the reader to judge Jude or his illusions. Hardy's attack on convention, the obstructive prejudice that thwarts Jude at every turn, has the effect of intensifying our sympathy for his desires even when they are delusory and unworthy. Thus we root for his admittance to Christminster even though it is a hopeless and even fraudulent dream, and we wish him happiness in his unconventional relationship with Sue, knowing that this love will dishearten and debilitate him. Our sympathy is greatly intensified at the end when the

"THREE YOUNG WOMEN WERE KNEELING"

narrative perspective becomes more or less singly focused on the tragic emotion of closure. Here we see a noble Jude who, in despair, achieves a tragic stature. He has no illusions, he is not weakened by self-accusation, he knows the bitterness of Job, but he still loves Sue, and his tragic stature elevates him and his love beyond censure.

Part First "At Marygreen": Hooked and Pizzled

Jude has a more or less consistent tone and a definite set of values throughout the opening five chapters. The many subtly muted allusions to Jesus help the reader to see young Jude as a sensitive, earnest, worthy young boy with strong spiritual yearnings. As he walks along the way to Christminster, "the white road seemed to ascend and diminish till it joined the sky. At the very top it was crossed at right angles by a green 'ridgeway' " (1:3). Flocks of sheep have been driven on this road with its cross in the sky. Jude's eyes then fall on a weather-beaten old barn where a roofer tells him that Christminster is sometimes visible at twilight "when the sun is going down in a blaze of flame." When the roofer cannot find a metaphor to describe the city, Jude suggests "the heavenly Jerusalem." Later, toward evening, when he is returning to the barn after the roofers have left, Jude thinks that "[p]erhaps if he prayed, the wish to see Christminster might be forwarded." He kneels on the third rung of the ladder and, praying, soon makes out points of light that turn out to be the spires, roof slates, and windows of the city. He gazes until the lights go out "like extinguished candles." Readers may be reminded of the scene in *Pilgrim's Progress* in which the shepherds of the Delectable Mountains point out to Christian the lights of the Celestial City in the distance.

The sacramental imagery and identification of Jude with Jesus, if hyperbolic, underscore Jude's sense of mission. This sense is established in the early chapters when as an 11-year-old he is in tears at the schoolmaster's departure from the village. At that point Christminster "acquired a tangibility, a permanence, and hold on his life" (1:3). His unformed resolve to follow Phillotson, to be a university graduate, and then to be ordained, is expressed as he stares into the village well at "a shining disk of quivering water" (1:1). Christminster will be his alma mater. Years later, he returns to this well in the "maddening torture" of his defeated dream, and remembering his earlier experience, he thinks "what a poor Christ he made" (2:7).

The coal carter introduces an ironical note of earthly humor. "Ah, young man," he says, sizing up Jude and noting that the book under his arm was merely stories for common folk, "[y]es, 'tis a serious-minded place. Not but there's wenches in the streets o' nights. . . . You know, I suppose, that they raise pa'sons there like radishes in a bed? And though it do take . . . five years to turn a lirruping hobble-de-hoy chap into a solemn preaching man with no corrupt passions, they'll do it, if it can be done, and polish un off like the workmen they be" (1:3). This sarcasm has the unmistakable stamp of wisdom. Whereas Jude's Christminster is a beautiful, visionary city, the real place is a fraud, unworthy of his longings and efforts. But this is yet to come, and the intensity of Jude's feelings makes him frown at the carter's levity. He flinches, as at ridicule. "It had been the yearning of his heart to find something to anchor on, to cling to—for some place which he could call admirable."

Jude, the child of an unhappy marriage, whose mother drowned herself, had been deposited one dark evening at the railway station in Alfredson and has been raised by a great aunt who does not want him. He has been attending night school as a special student, for school is a luxury for an 11-year-old pensioner like him, who ought to be earning his keep. He has a deep feeling for helpless creatures, suffers despondent reflections on the cruelty of life, and believes that growing up warps a person. He is a lonely boy who is "crazy for books" (1:2) and desperate for something and someone to believe in and love, the sort of person "who was born to ache a good deal before the fall of the curtain upon his unnecessary life should signify that all was well with him again." This melancholy foreshadowing translates eventually into Jude's despairing cry, "Let the day perish wherein I was born" (6:11).

What kind of character is Jude? In the opening chapters he is a high-minded idealist with deep spiritual needs, the kind of person who is resilient and persevering. But an ironic undercurrent runs through these opening chapters and makes a different impression: that Jude is not a potential hero but a casualty of the social and mental restlessness of his time. This idea is suggested in the opening pages where Hardy describes with distaste the effect of progress on the rural world. In Marygreen, where everything but the wellshaft has been pulled down and replaced by utilitarian and cheap products, Jude's restlessness and ambition are identified with the social forces that are obliterating the old world and its morality. This countertheme indicates that he is not an exceptional person driven by deep spiritual needs to shape his future but a victim of history. Because he is caught between two worlds, between one class and another, between disbelief and free thinking, he is perhaps even a fool. The subtle undercurrent, that he is a fool, bound to aims that are unreal, eventually turns into parody and snide authorial comment.

The emblem of the old morality is Vilbert, an extraordinarily thin man with a tall hat and swallowtail coat, swinging along on long thin legs and noiseless boots. His movements about the countryside are "as truly timed as those of the planets in their courses" (1:4), but his figure is like the pendulum of a clock that is winding down. He is an anachronism, a cartoon image of the old order, in contrast to little Father Time, who is the emblem of the new valueless millennium, a future of meaningless chaos. Vilbert, who is superseded by the new science, excites Jude's interest, only to callously rebutt him—a parallel to Jude's relationship with Christminster.

Because Vilbert stands for the old order, he is also an emblem of Christianity. In making Vilbert a physician to the poor, but a charlatan healer, Hardy exposes Christianity as a fable. Vilbert dispenses medicines that "could only be obtained from a particular animal which grazed on Mount Sinai" and proclaims himself "the only proprietor of those celebrated pills that infallibly cure" (1:4). From Christminster, one of his centers, Vilbert recruits Jude, making him a believer in his infallible pills. No food for the soul is to be found in this ministry, no intellectual life, only rejection and bitter disappointment. In short, physician Vilbert represents the culture of Christminster and the social institutions and laws buttressed by Christianity; although he is a comic figure, he appears in moments of reversal and misfortune, giving the triumphant stamp of the old morality to Jude's despair.

Jude cries bitterly over Vilbert's broken promise to give him Greek and Latin grammars. Even the discovery that years of plodding lie between him and a poor proficiency in the ancient tongues does not discourage him; instead he worships Christminster even more. Hardy displays Jude as a baker's boy delivering loaves in the early morning and trying to make out passages from Cicero, Virgil, and Horace with the use of a dictionary. But an inbred chasteness in his nature makes him, at 16, suppress his interest in pagan literature, thus checking, by implication, the awakening of his sexuality. He limits himself to studying the gospels and epistles in the Greek New Testament. His heart afire for the university, he decides to learn a trade that will enable him to maintain himself in Christminster, and he apprentices himself to a church builder in Alfredson who teaches him to restore the masonry of village churches.

A Reading of the Text

In his nineteenth year Jude takes pride in his progress. He has made do with very little in the way of books and has had no formal education, but he has learned some mathematics and Roman history and has a little proficiency in Latin and Greek. He counts on hiring qualified tutors and gaining admittance into one of the colleges, where he dreams of becoming a scholar and ascetic, "leading a pure, energetic, wise, Christian life" (1:6). His dream is to be a Doctor of Divinity, and he secretly fantasizes himself an archdeacon, even a bishop. "Yes, Christminster shall be my Alma Mater; and I'll be her beloved son, in whom she shall be well pleased." The allusion to St. Matthew's gospel accentuates the sense of mission.

At this point Arabella enters Jude's life, waking him from his dreaminess. She flings a pig's penis at him, which catches him smartly on the ear. There is mockery in his being smacked with a pig's pizzle in the midst of his "magnificent Christminster dream" (1:6). Hardy laughs uncomfortably at the mischief that will be caused in Jude's life when his lower passions are roused: Jude has selected Arabella "in commonplace obedience to conjunctive orders from headquarters, unconsciously received by unfortunate men when the last intention of their lives is to be occupied with the feminine." The bureaucratic language expresses the authority of sexuality; suddenly eight years of dedicated study are of no importance at all. Jude stops to make Arabella's acquaintance, although his intellectual eye sees for a fleeting moment "something in her quite antipathetic" to his spiritual strivings.

Stench and gruntings from her father's piggeries surround him as he pays court. In a tone that is tongue-in-cheek with a wry distasteful wrinkle on the nose, Hardy expresses not mockery at Jude's dreams but vexation at life's tricks and the deceptions of false dimples, false hair, and false pregnancy: "Jude, the incipient scholar, prospective D.D., Professor, Bishop, or what not, felt himself honoured and glorified by the condescension of this handsome country wench in agreeing to take a walk with him in her Sunday frock and ribbons" (1:7). The little town on fire to the north of the Brownhouse represents the hallowed city of his dreams going up in smoke. The picture of Samson and Delilah on the tavern wall evokes the story of a man with a mission who is emasculated by a woman. Jude is betraying his dream; he is caught, to use Milton's language, in the snare of "a lascivious concubine." The book on his desk when he returns to it reproaches him "like the unclosed eyes of a dead man" gone blank—like Jude's mind.

Yet at the same time that Jude is an agreeable little boy playing at being grown up, he is also a very immature 19-year-old for a sensual woman to chase. The escape of three unfattened pigs from their sty introduces a farcical passage in which Jude is like the runaway being pursued by Arabella. It is a recurring perspective on their relationship. Arabella will run him down again, entrapping him again, and be unsatisfied again. Here, however, in the first flush of the first courtship, the parody is free of bitterness. " 'O dear, how hot I be!' Without relinquishing her hold of Jude's hand she swerved aside and flung herself down on the sod under a stunted thorn, precipitately pulling Jude on to his knees at the same time" (1:8). Her body calls him to her, "heaving and falling in quick pants, her face flushed, her full red lips parted, and a fine dew of perspiration on her skin." But the would-be Doctor of Divinity is as uncomprehending as the stunted thorn.

The narrative asides become increasingly acerbic—Jude is remiss, Jude is neglectful of his high purpose—as the parody of the courtship advances to the black comedy of the pig sticking. Inevitably, determined that she rather than Christminster will possess Jude, Arabella gets him to sleep with her. "[W]ith a jealous, tigerish indrawing of breath" she lures him to her bed, and Jude is shorn of his dignity. Once he is compromised into marrying her—Arabella pretends to be pregnant and possibly half believes in the fertility potion Vilbert has given her—the narrative turns tawdry, and a tone of bitterness and invective emerges in Hardy's asides.

Hardy so accentuates the gruesomeness of the pig sticking after Jude and Arabella's wedding that it appears that he intends to depict something more than a difference in sensibilities. Jude's waking passion has been identified with pigs, and more generally with the perception that striving is futile. In chapter 2 he lies down beside a pigsty and, staring through the interstices of his hat, ponders the cruelty of nature. He reflects on how life stunts a person and wishes that he did not have to grow up. The striving will is always thwarted in Hardy, and sexual appetite is its nemesis. In likening Jude and Arabella's marriage to a pig sticking, Hardy degrades marriage, but more than that, he portrays sex as a disgusting and spirit-denying act. Being married to Arabella is to be stuck properly, to be "well bled . . . to die slow." The rage and despair inherent in the death of Jude's high purpose is expressed by the "dismal, sordid, ugly spectacle—to those who saw it as other than an ordinary obtaining of meat" (1:10).

Yet the pig sticking has been read by Arthur Mizener as a burlesque of Duncan's murder in *Macbeth*, with the pig substituting for the king.[2] Arabella says, "Well—you must do the sticking—there's no help for it." And later, "I'll show you how. Or I'll do it myself" (1:10). Jude agrees, and when he is revolted by the pig's wail of despair, she prods him. "Don't be such a tender-hearted fool! There's the sticking-knife—the one with the point." Mizener considers the pig's death scene "sentimental." The pig's "glazing eyes [rivet] themselves on Arabella with the eloquently keen reproach of a creature recognizing at last the treachery of those who had seemed his only friends." The scene is both gruesomely funny and a satire on Jude's pretentions.

Jude's relationship with Arabella mixes tragedy and farce: whereas Jude swears allegiance to the noble muses, Arabella says, "hoity-toity" and dirties his books with pig fat. Later, to humiliate him for botching the slaughter, and to mock his scholarly pretensions, she disarrays her hair and clothes and stomps about the roadside proclaiming to passers-by on their way to church that her would-be parson has taken to beating her. She is larger than life—a woman who tosses a pig's genitals at a man to catch his attention, hides an egg between her breasts to invite his pursuit, and entraps him with a fake pregnancy. She is vulgar, conniving, selfish, yet she also has earthy, humorous common sense. She is resilient, a survivor, and her perspective is always reliable.

The point of view that constantly shifts from sympathy to mockery, and the occasional switches from close to distant perspective mean that the ethical, social, and philosophic inferences are always changing. In the long view, what does it matter if one is bespattered by matrimony or crushed by some other accidental catastrophe that befalls those who attempt to make something of their lives? In the near view, Hardy shuttles between farce and high seriousness, both of which contain bitter indignation, for in the near view, the outcome matters terribly. Indignation turns the light farce of Jude's courtship into the black comedy of the pig sticking; it breaks out in authorial asides against the institution of holy wedlock, and it highlights Jude's failure, shackled to an unsuitable woman and imprisoned by his poverty. When Jude decides to kill himself by walking out onto the frozen pond, in despair of Christminster and his old high purpose, our sympathy for him is muted by Hardy's perfunctory depiction. Hardy is not comfortable with Jude, in this scene, either as a fool or as a hero.

But the pig sticking and attempted suicide can be read yet another way. Lawrence says that Hardy, though the most sensuous of English writers, was incapable of weaning himself from Christianity's abhorrence of the flesh. Thus Jude's entrapment in the degradation of the flesh causes his despair. Yet at the same time Hardy shows the tragic consequences of austerity in his male characters. Clym Yeobright (*The Return of the Native*) and Angel Clare (*Tess of the d'Urbervilles*), for example, are incapable of loving women because they are driven to serve some idea at the expense of their own sensual natures. But Arabella, the embodiment of sensuality—robust, disgusting, vital, and conniving—saves Jude from being stunted by the cerebral side of his nature; she saves Jude from the fate of Clym and Angel—from becoming, that is, the bodiless counterpart to his cousin Sue. That she is a pig killer's daughter, rather coarse and fleshy, and given to using tricks to catch her man, Lawrence ascribes to Hardy's ambivalence, to his mental aversion to the flesh.

To Lawrence, Sue and Jude are victims of centuries of Christianity. J. I. M. Stewart tacitly acknowledges this reading when he speaks of "some principle of sexual revulsion" (Stewart, 196) that is at the bottom of Arabella's desertion of Jude. She is "not a fool" Stewart says, and we must suppose that she has good ground for writing him off (Stewart, 197). The unpleasant graphic coarseness of the pig sticking supports this idea when read as an expression of Jude's revulsion from the physical and the sexual.

Lawrence's idea has also been developed by Philip Weinstein. Jude, he says, has a clog. He cannot grasp life between his knees. He is a born loser, a futile dreamer. When he stomps on the ice, it is as if in some central part of his being he was a spirit "stunned to find [himself] placed on earth and embodied in flesh" (Weinstein, 131–32).

PART SECOND "AT CHRISTMINSTER": AN INVISIBLE MAN

At the end of Part First, the halo of light above Christminster has become "a small dim nebulousness, hardly recognizable save by the eye of faith" (1:11). Jude enters the city on foot at the beginning of Part Second, "a forcible, meditative, and earnest" man of 22 (2:1), seeking temporary employment as a stonecutter adept at renovative work on churches. Dedicated as ever to the old idea, Jude rents a room in a suburb and hurries at evening to the precincts of the university, lingering caressingly against the walls and buildings. There he feels the eerie sensation of being invisible, a ghostly presence, as he conjures up ghostly sons of the university—Jonson, Browning, Swinburne, Newman, Keble, Pusey, Bolingbroke, and Gibbon—all of them, in his mind, "the spirits of just men made perfect" (Hebrews 12:23). The irony that pervades this scene emphasizes Jude's naive absorption in a destructive and illusory dream, in which not only the dead, but also the living, are perfect.

Hardy says, "Necessary meditations on the actual, including the mean bread-and-cheese question, dissipated the phantasmal for a while, and compelled Jude to smother high thinkings under immediate needs" (2:2). But Hardy's sarcasm also implies that Christminster is a fraud, "pompous," irrelevant, "barbaric"—barbaric because it is a bulwark of social prejudice and has a hostile spirit to workingmen like Jude. Jude will always be a spectre, invisible in his workingman's blouse to those complacently engaged in the proceedings of the university. There is a moment, Hardy says, when Jude comprehends the reality of Christminster and has "a true illumination; that here in the

"'SEE HOW HE'S SERVED ME!' SHE CRIED"

stone yard was a centre of effort as worthy as that dignified by the name of scholarly study within the noblest of the colleges. But he lost it under stress of his old idea." He refuses to make a career of stone-work, and Hardy calls his dedication to the dream of gaining admittance to one of the colleges "his form of the modern vice of unrest."

Why does Hardy blame Jude's thirst for knowledge on the destructive influence of social forces? Why is he critical of Jude's efforts to direct his life toward higher learning? Why does he imply that self-discontent motivates him to reach beyond his class? If Christminster were worthy of his efforts, would he still be doomed to fail? From one perspective, Jude is puzzling his way out of the labyrinth of nineteenth-century thought, with its oppressive institutions, conventions, and morality. But Hardy also portrays Jude as a victim of his own personal history.

Sue's role as substitute for Christminster in Jude's life is indicated by the abruptness of the transition from his obsession with his dream to his kissing her photograph. Hardy prepares this role for her when as a boy of 11 Jude's aunt speaks of the two of them in one breath, linking them as offspring of bad marriages and as lovers of books. The photograph itself is identified with Christminster; Jude spies it at his aunt's house between two brass candlesticks on the mantle, the "pretty girlish face" of his cousin enshrined like the city of his dreams, with a halo made by the impression of her broad hat's radiating folds (2:1).

Jude's projects fail, says Weinstein, because Jude is fickle, readily substituting one dream for another. He is unfit for reality, negating whatever he can actually experience. The projects he embarks on "either fail to meet the conditions of daily life or—meeting them—produce ennui and then disabling fatigue." Jude, and Hardy's striving characters in general, "have sufficient energy to scorn the available, not to create alternatives; and this is so, one finally gathers, because their imagination is stocked with nothing but unrealities" (Weinstein, 131). Hence Jude's story is one of reversals and failures.

To Weinstein, Hardy's point of view toward Jude is consistent. Hardy, he asserts, constantly disparages Jude's idealism, portraying the pathos and hopelessness of dreamers who never take control of their lives. Indeed, he says, Jude (absenting himself from the hard necessities of living), often lapses into a schizoid frame of mind wherein he muses and pines for fraudulent goals. His campaign to get into Christminster is so blundering and absent-minded "that no reader can be surprised by its failure" (Weinstein, 132). He enters the city at night and hears "its medley of disembodied voices" (Weinstein, 122), because he himself is ghostly and abstract in his relation to his sought-after culture. Eventually, Jude dies unenlightened, having never confronted his complicity in his downfall.

Other critics interpret Hardy's multiple points of view in terms that allow for the novel's powerful emotional impact. Patricia Ingham, calling *Jude* "the most powerful indictment of the sexual and class oppression of its time" (Ingham, xxii), says that the ambiguity reflects Hardy's struggle to express hostility toward the middle-class values that repressed aspiring workingmen and independent women. His attempts to break free from his own values—represented by his shifting from approval to hostility toward the orthodoxies of his day—reveal a pattern "in which an apparent success is always followed by regression" (Ingham, xx). The novel also enacts Hardy's inner struggle as he worked to create a revolutionary art that subverts the whole of established society. The ambiguity records the zigzag course of this struggle, the fluctuations of Hardy's success and regression.

Peter Widdowson holds that Hardy created characters who are "ideologically and socially determined, 'circumstanced' by the subject-positions they occupy" because Hardy was powerless to change his own origins (Widdowson, 213). Consequently, in contrast to Weinstein, Widdowson believes that Hardy does not blame Jude for the mistakes he makes; instead he engulfs Jude's life in an aura of gloom and pessimism.

Both Norman Page and Terry Eagleton conclude that Hardy's shifting point of view is an ironic device for revealing Jude's stumbling growth. "[I]n the novel," Eagleton argues, "the relation between ideals and harsh actuality is a dialectical one: the ideal criticises the reality but is in turn exposed by it as limited or utopian. (Thus the novel's original title, 'The Simpletons,' is both an irony at the expense of the society and a comment on the nature of Jude and Sue's idealism)."[3] Both Eagleton and Page focus on Jude's struggle to conquer his susceptibility to illusion. Once Jude is awakened to the reality of Victorian prejudice, "[he] refuses to back down from the question of his own identity" almost to the bitter end (Eagleton, 64, 66).

Jude is as far from gaining admittance to Christminster "as if he had been at the antipodes" (2:2), because no matter how courageous and determined he is, he cannot conquer social prejudice. Yet the image of Jude huddling over his books in a coat and gloves on a cold night contradicts Hardy's frequently snide insinuations that he is a fool. Why should he live on bread alone? That Christminster is fraudulent is independent of the fact that poverty prevents his class from aiming high; thus if Jude avoids acknowledging the obstacle of class prejudice, it is to sustain his life-giving illusions. Sue emerges when the practical realization of the Christminster dream recedes. "A sweet, saintly, Christian business, hers!" he thinks (2:2), on spying her illuminating the word "alleluia" on zinc—an ironic thought about the free-thinking Sue. He hears a "softened and sweetened" version of himself in the accents of her voice: she, instead of Christminster, will ennoble him.

In Hardy's autobiographical *Life*, he notes for April 1888 the idea for a short story about "a young man—'who could not go to Oxford'—His struggles and ultimate failure. Suicide. There is something the world ought to be shown, and I am the one to show it to them" (*Life*, 216). Probably Hardy shifted from Jude's frustrated academic ambitions to his frustrated love for Sue because focusing on Jude's pursuit of an academic career would have necessitated giving life to Christminster, and this was a dead end. Moreover, as Hardy delved with increasing complexity into his hero's striving for a destructively alluring dream, he felt encouraged to substitute Sue for Christminster. It enabled him to lavish his artistry on a love story while symbolically maintaining his original conception. For Sue, like the university, is a labyrinth of contradictions: the serpent Error coils in her heart. Christminster is an anomaly: it is a great center of culture built around the scholarship of learned men who greet new scientific thought yet cannot break free from the nooses of their education and the Bible. Sue resembles one of those Doctors of Divinity who has been won over by the new thought. Intellectually she is a total unbeliever. She thinks she is a liberated thinker, a neopagan, a reader of Swinburne, Mill, Gibbon, and other heterodox writers, yet she turns out to be like Christminster, a prisoner of convention, deadlocked between the old world and the new. And like the university, she frustrates Jude's passion for human fulfillment.

For Jude, Sue is always an object of infinite romance like the university, especially after his Christminster dream collapses. She is, Alvarez says, "the untouched part of him, all intellect, nerves, and sensitivity, essentially bodiless;" it is "this combination of nonphysical purity with exaggeratedly sharp intellect and sensitivity which preserves her for Jude as an object of ideal yearning, hopeless and debilitating. It is a yearning for his own lost innocence, before his Christminster ambitions were diverted by Arabella" (Alvarez, 116).

When Jude first meets Sue, he is reading with "indescribable enchantment" the Greek of I Corinthians 8:6: "but to us there is but one God, the Father, of whom are all things, and we in him." Jude becomes preoccupied with Sue, experiencing "a fearful bliss in doing what was erratic, informal, and unexpected" (2:4). Thus begins the first movement of a dance that is the central feature of the tragedy, Jude and Sue ultimately exchanging positions—his views growing, hers grotesquely narrowing (Stewart, 193).

"The pretty, liquid-eyed, light-footed young woman Sue Bridehead" (2:3) is first presented in symbolic poses. Out walking, she sees Christminster over her shoulder, "the most Christian city in the country," and before her she sees, with his wares sparkling in a brilliant sun, a dark-haired huckster of pagan statuary, from whom she purchases a Venus and an Apollo. "When she handled them the white pipeclay came off on her gloves and jacket." She lies to her landlady, telling her that the wrapped figures are St. Peter and Mary Magdalen. In these ways Hardy suggests the tenuousness of her free thinking. When she displays her nude statuary in her room, a print of Jesus on the cross stands between them.

There is a fatalistic bleakness in the structure of part 2, chapter 5, where Hardy creates a double panel in which Sue succumbs to Phillotson's advances although she finds his desire distasteful, and Jude muses on a model of Jerusalem at the time of the Crucifixion. Like subliminal flashes, these images foretell the end of the story—Sue's degradation and Jude's death. The early glimpses of her in front of the model of Jerusalem reinforce the idea of deadlock between the mind and the emotions. She is outspokenly critical of the model, receives the mildest of remonstrances from Phillotson, who is plainly flirting with her, and turns her guilt at having spoken audaciously and irreverently into aggression against herself. Feeling the need to repent, she later draws for Phillotson a faithful reproduction of the artist's model that she had ridiculed. When she becomes engaged to Phillotson, her choice seems to be the penance of a free spirit, the first step toward her ultimate penance, her grotesque efforts to be a conventional wife and a good Christian. Where is the critic of Christminster, the free spirit, the Shelleyan rebel, in the docile young woman who walks with Phillotson beneath an umbrella, his arm about her waist?

Sue's engagement startles Jude and alerts him to the probability of hovering about the walls of the university indefinitely. When Jude tells a Marygreen neighbor he cannot afford college, the neighbor remarks, "Just what we thought! Such places be not for such as you—only for them with plenty of money" (2:6). This country advice sounds like wisdom to him. No arm will be wondrously stretched out from the colleges to place Jude in "a seat in the paradise of the learned." Jude's dreams and schemes burst "like an iridescent soap-bubble," the point underscored by his remembering Heine's couplet, "Above the youth's inspired and flashing eyes / I see the motley mocking fool's-cap rise!" Although Jude's academic effort is hopeless, Hardy indicts the system when Jude fails, receiving a brutal rejection from the master of Biblioll College: "Sir—I have read your letter with interest; and, judging from your description of yourself as a working-man, I venture to think that you will have a much better chance of success in life by remaining in your own sphere and sticking to your trade than by adopting any other course. That, therefore, is what I advise you to do. Yours faithfully, T. Tetuphenay." That the closed-minded, closed-door Master of Biblioll College is named Tetuphenay is either an allusion to Molière's religious hypocrite, Tartuffe, or a reference to the Greek word "*tetythenai*," meaning "to have beaten." His letter might well be translated into the elitist sentiment of Dr. Johnson: "Sir, we permit cows in a meadow but we drive them out of the garden."[4]

Jude finds no consolation in the reflection that there would be no seat of learning without stonemasons like him, nor does he relieve his torment by considering "that the town life was a book of humanity infinitely more palpitating, varied, and compendious than the gown life."

How should he take solace from this illumination? Being young, he can only express his grief in grand gestures. On the wall of the college from which he had been rejected Jude scrawls the verse "I have understanding as well as you; I am not inferior to you: yea, who knoweth not such things as these?" (Job 12:3). The next evening he blasphemes the Nicene creed[5] by reciting it in Latin for shots of hard liquor in the manner of a priest leading a congregation, and he provokes in himself a characteristic reaction: the same devastating feeling of worthlessness that led him onto the ice after the breakup of his marriage carries him to Sue for consolation. "O, do anything with me, Sue—kill me—I don't care!" he says when he comes to her later that night. "Only don't hate me and despise me like all the rest of the world!" (2:7).

The masters of the colleges are impervious to the criticism of Benjamin Jowett, professor of Greek at Oxford, that the narrow letter of orthodoxy perverts their admission standards. "It would be a strange and almost incredible thing that the Gospel, which at first made war only on the vices of mankind, should now be opposed to one of the highest and rarest of human virtues—the love of truth. And that in the present day the great object of Christianity should be, not to change the lives of men, but to prevent them from changing their opinions; that would be a singular inversion of the purposes for which Christ came into the world."[6]

It would be the mark of Jude's coming of age if he finally learned to criticize Christminster in the spirit of Jowett without self-recrimination. In his retreat from the city that had been a "thorn in his side," Jude sits down by a well, weary and mud-bespattered, thinking of "what a poor Christ he made" (2:7). He has been betrayed by society in its holiest enclave. After the humiliation of facing his aunt, which drives the last nail into his cross, he sleeps a short while. He wakes "as if he had awakened in hell," which is where Hardy leaves him. By dropping the Christ allusion at this point Hardy implies that Jude will remain among the abandoned, waiting in "unhope."

PART THIRD "AT MELCHESTER": COUSIN SUE'S BEST MAN

Let us look at the novel, as Ramon Saldivar and Philip Weinstein do, as a structure of reversals and failure, of illusions and disappointments, in which Jude postures melodramatically when his dreams are shattered by reality. In Part Third, chapter 1, Jude purges himself of his religious ambitions, cheering himself up by casting out his vain and hopeless dream of entering the church as an ordained minister. His

"JUDE STOOD UP AND BEGAN RHETORICALLY"

ideal, he thinks, has been admirable but futile and had degenerated into selfishness. He, and thousands like him, are victims of the changing times, of "a social unrest which had no foundation in the nobler instincts" (3:1). If he is passionate in his Christianity, why does he not enter the Church as a licentiate and serve as a "humble curate wearing his life out in an obscure village or city slum"? Lowering his ideal seems better to him than pursuing his fond, foolish dream of becoming a bishop. And yet the new desire does not rally his soul. Shabby, lonely, humble to the nod of townfolk who condescend to give him menial odd jobs, Jude begins to drift, and he might have gone on drifting had not Sue summoned him to Melchester, where there just happened to be a theological college. Thanks to Sue his more modest scheme of pursuing his apostolic career is revived. He is inspired by the romantic calculation that like Christ he might begin his ministry at the age of 30, "an age which much attracted him as being that of his exemplar when he first began to teach in Galilee" (3:1).

Although Jude's search for meaning in his love for Sue will end in tragedy, it begins as a gentle burlesque; in merely substituting Sue for Christminster he is blind again to a new folly. Sue Bridehead, his new and absorbing dream, is in some respects more a phenomenon than a character. She is as ambiguous and as potent to Hardy as Christminster. Sue has been described by Marlene Springer as "a woman with a twentieth-century mind controlled by a nineteenth-century view of self,"[7] and her conflicts and evasions dramatize the deadlock of a transitional consciousness. Her aversion to sex may derive from a socially conditioned association of eroticism with sin. The pattern of her behavior—aggression turned inward in penance for social defiance—suggests that denying oneself pleasure is a fitting punishment for free thinking. Thus, she rejects marriage in order to avoid being shackled by oppressive convention, but she experiences guilt in the form of frigidity. According to Terry Eagleton, "[h]er freedom, as a result, is in part negative and destructive—a self-possessive individualism which sees all permanent commitment as imprisoning, a fear of being possessed which involves a fear of giving" (Eagleton, 66). To Eagleton, Sue exemplifies the odds against attempting "to live authentically in a false society" (Eagleton, 70). The story of Sue and Jude's love contrasts Jude's resistance to self-censure with Sue's collapse into convention. "There is no need for this society to crush those who make the break for freedom," Eagleton observes; "the roots of its deathly ideology sink sufficiently deep in the mind for the self to act as its own censor, anxiously desiring its own extinction" (Eagleton, 70).

Kathleen Blake reads Sue as a passionate woman who restrains her sexuality to achieve personal emancipation. Sue practices sexual repression to avoid the prison of matrimony and to widen her opportunities; her ambition is to live with men while escaping them. Contact with men is necessary both for the advantages they offer and for the sexual stimulation that enlivens her mind. Sue is not frigid, but she has learned to reroute her sexuality so that she feels energy without feeling desire. In her attempt to live as a free woman she toys with Jude. Blake contends that "[t]he feminism by which Sue frees her brilliant individuality" threatens to make her a "frigid woman," yet her feminism "keeps her in constant peril of the 'femaleness that breaks her.' "[8] To Blake, Sue is a pioneer, trying to save herself from the demeaning prostitution of marriage, but Jude's love for her compromises her desperate efforts and brings on their tragedy.

From another perspective, Sue is not exceptional and her collapse is not a social indictment. She is a nonconformist because she finds sex repugnant. Equality between the sexes does not interest her. She has no cause other than self-interest. Her gripe against the institution of marriage is that the pressure of a husband's desire will expose "the full, bitter sterility of her narcissism" (Alvarez, 118). Robert Heilman thinks that Sue is an example of "the danger of trying to live by rationality alone"—that her nervous self-enclosure and frigidity result from her struggle against the "simmering revolt" of her emotions and needs.[9] From this perspective Sue is a neurotic woman and Jude's love for her diminishes his stature: he is not a tragic figure, but a mild, civil, lonely man who never finds peace and never comprehends why he is on bad terms with life. His misfortunes and death have no social significance.

Sue has no qualms about summoning Jude to Melchester despite her engagement to Phillotson. At the castle, on the day of her outing from the training school, she studies Jude's expression when he is looking at paintings of Christian martyrs and saints: "It was evident that her cousin deeply interested her, as one might be interested in a man puzzling out his way along a labyrinth from which one had one's self escaped" (3:2). Because she understands that convention is merely controlled opinion, Irving Howe calls her "promethean in mind."[10] Yet it also appears that she has no concern for Jude's real needs or well-being, and that in the role of enlightener to her cousin she controls the relationship, inhibiting his expression of feeling while enjoying the thrill of being loved.

It may be that the sensitive shepherd in whose hut they spend the night represents Hardy's visceral reaction against the frigid purity of his heroine. The conversation in the hut displays the contradiction in Sue's character. She has left the training school for her outing attired like a nun in her uniform and expects severe consequences for staying out the whole night, but as she shares dinner with Jude, the shepherd, and his mother, she is exhilarated. She feels "[o]utside all laws except gravitation and germination" (3:2). Her buoyancy irritates Jude; he sees it as emotional hypocrisy. Heartsore at the thought of her engagement to Phillotson, Jude accuses her of being an ordinary product of city culture—"[a]n urban miss is what you are." Protesting that he is wrong and that she is "[t]he Ishmaelite," she asserts, "I crave to get back to the life of my infancy and its freedom."

Kathleen Blake says that Sue intends to remain a child, that is, a virgin, so that she can emancipate herself from the misfortune of being born a woman and gain some control over her life. According to Blake, independent women like Sue must be Ishmaelites and children in order to escape the fate of Victorian women, who through matrimony suffered a terrible tyranny at the hands of men (Blake, 86).

The diptychlike structure of the chapter in which Sue is punished by the training school and escapes to Jude enlists our sympathy for Sue by setting her apart from her 70 classmates.

> [E]very face [in the classroom bore] the legend "The Weaker" upon it, as the penalty of the sex wherein they were moulded, which by no possible exertion of their willing hearts and abilities could be made strong while the inexorable laws of nature remain what they are. They formed a pretty, suggestive, pathetic sight, of whose pathos and beauty they were themselves unconscious, and would not discover till, amid the storms and strains of after-years, with their injustice, loneliness, child-bearing, and bereavement, their minds would revert to this experience. (3:3)

Sue tells Jude, as she sits in his armchair with her underclothes drying before his fire, "[m]y life has been entirely shaped by what people call a peculiarity in me. I have no fear of men, as such, nor of their books. I have mixed with them—one or two of them particularly—almost as one of their own sex" (3:4). She makes a point of adding that she does not fear sexual pressure because she never gives men any sexual encouragement. She then tells him that for 15 months she had lived with a Christminster graduate who became ill because she would not sleep with him: "He said I was breaking his heart by holding out against him so long at such close quarters; he could never have believed it of woman. . . . His death caused a terrible remorse in me for my cruelty." The "contralto note of tragedy coming suddenly into her silvery voice" on seeing the effect of her words on Jude may be a warning, or a plea, or coquetry. She tells him she is a virgin but adds indignantly that she is not cold by nature: "Some of the most passionately erotic poets have been the most self-contained in their daily lives," she says, and she pleads with him in a voice of "extraordinary tenderness" not to be vexed with her.

Sue has been highly stimulated by her adventure. She has jumped from a window and waded across a creek up to her shoulders; she faces expulsion from the school and will have much to explain to her fiancé; furthermore she has put herself in a compromising situation with her cousin, who adores her. Possibly the crossed signals she is giving him are the result of her nerve-strained state. So when Jude, depressed by her apparent indifference to his feelings, suppresses his desire and talks about becoming a minister, her contempt for his ambitions may derive from agitation. She has no religion, and she thinks Jude should have learned from his Christminster experience. How, after being "elbowed off the pavement by the millionaires' sons," could he still be blind to what Christminster and the Church were, a meritocracy of "fetichists and ghost-seers" (3:4)? Maybe Sue does not know her own feelings when she denounces the allegorical chapter headings to the "Song of Solomon" as attempts to "plaster over with ecclesiastical abstractions such ecstatic, natural, human love as lies in that great and passionate song!" She seems to want Jude to respond to her sexually. Her attack on Christianity, on the goal of Jude's striving and dreaming for a dozen years, forces him to defend his faith despite her excitable state, and this provokes her to tears and accusations that he is "on the side of the people in the Training School." She demands absolute loyalty from Jude—insisting that he choose between her and the Church fathers. But her attack has nothing to do with Christminster and the Song of Solomon; rather it is an oblique play for love. When Jude does speak to her of his love, she replies in her "softest note of severity" that he is not to speak of it now. Then, feeling guilty for having manipulated him, she explains her behavior in a way that puts a good face on it. She says that she has wanted to "ennoble some man to high aims." Then she makes another stab at his cherished beliefs: "[b]ut you take so much tradition on trust." Thus she implies that if he wants to be her comrade, he should put his trust in her, not in fetichists and ghost-seers.

Philip Weinstein says that both Jude and Sue cannot tolerate emotional tension and that they use language to evade rather than to clarify their confusion. Jude and Sue are alienated; their world has "become unmoored from [its] natural certitude" (Weinstein, 130). Since they still believe in the old truths, the words they use to try to make sense of their feelings are drawn from "a cultural stockpile" that cannot express their needs. Later they rely on one external voice after another, turning language into "an incoherent amalgam of the commonplaces of their culture" (Weinstein, 121). They are condemned never to understand the reasons for their alienation because, as Weinstein argues, Hardy was incapable of making them far-seeing and truly tragic.

In his reading of literature as a mirror of culture, D. H. Lawrence observed that as Christianity became less of a social and political force its covert hold on the individual became destructive. In writers from Aristophanes to Chaucer, lustiness and bawdiness were commonplace, and notions of sin and guilt in regard to sex did not prevail. But during the Renaissance, a paralysis of fear, "a terror, almost a horror of sexual life," gripped the consciousness of northern Europe (*Phoenix*, 551). Dante was only "slightly dishonorable" in worshipping Beatrice while he kept hidden a "cosy bifurcated wife" in his bed.[11] By the time of Milton, a mental-spiritual consciousness triumphed over the instincts; a life-denying mode of behavior became moral, based on glorification of the mind and disgust for the body. In his *Study of Thomas Hardy* Lawrence describes Sue Bridehead as a character who embodies the final act of this tragedy: Sue is the result of centuries of "ultra-Christian" training, a woman "born with the vital female atrophied in her" (*Phoenix*, 416). She vamps Jude so that she can have, in Lawrence's terms, a spiritual marriage—"bodiless"—with a man who "could receive this drainage, receiving nothing back again" while he gives her the mental stimulus of "constant jeopardy" (*Phoenix*, 498). Sue induges in this spiritual vampirism because, despite herself, she has become Jude's nemesis, modern woman's revenge on her lover for his weakness and for the "deadly anarchy in her own being" (*Phoenix*, 497).

In the sequence of events leading up to Sue's marriage, she and Jude are actors in a ghoulish farce. She alternates between telling him he must not love her and telling him that he may. She blames her expulsion on his love and bursts into jealous tears when she hears that he is married to Arabella, stamping her foot and crying, "it is perfectly damnable how things are" (3:6). She behaves like a vindictive adolescent, promptly writing him after her outburst that she has fixed the date for her marriage to Phillotson—"[w]ish me joy"—and follows with a second letter requesting that Jude "give her away" (3:7). The narrative becomes silly, the lovers' antics absurd, when Jude offers the engaged couple his lodgings in Melchester and Sue responds by coming to live with him for the 10-day period of residence before the wedding.

Jude adores her and plays his farcical part in the preposterous hope that she will elope with him. She is out of control—spun about between two bad alternatives, and feeling threatened. She wants neither marriage to Phillotson nor passion from Jude. If only Jude were not married; if only he could love her without animal desire—these hopes create the conflict that makes her vindictive. As the day of her marriage to Phillotson nears, she looks for ways to hurt Jude: she comes to live with him before the wedding, and then on the morning of the wedding, she takes Jude's arm and walks up and down the church aisle with him as if they were the engaged couple rehearsing the ceremony.

Kathleen Blake says her behavior is a manifestation of rerouted sexuality: "Since she does not feel desire directly, she invents original and 'perverse' substitutes" (Blake, 95); in this way Sue directs the sexual stimulation she requires into relatively safe channels. Hardy treats all this in a whimsical style. The narrative has become farce, yet the characters' emotions and complex psychologies are treated in earnest. Does Hardy's grin express the self-deception of his characters? Philip Weinstein says their conversation is "like cartoon utterances, cascading like soap-bubbles from the already finished figures who remain mute beside their utterance" (Weinstein, 122).

Perhaps Hardy is implying that Sue is innocent, that she does not understand her own behavior. And yet her command, "Wish me joy. Remember I say you are to," and her request, "Jude, will you give me away," flash in the sunlight like blades or fangs. She savors Jude's mortification. She pretends there is something noble about her eccentric behavior in the church. After all, ordinary people do not have the courage to act as Sue does. Yet obviously her motive is to hurt him: "I shall walk down the church like this with my husband in about two hours, shan't I!" (3:7). She is really distressed by the evidence of his suffering, but her distress is based on self-deception. She "[blinks] away an access of eye moisture," which is as artificial a way of saying "tears" as her contrition is genuine. By exaggerating Sue's experience, Hardy ridicules her. The whole scene teeters on a parody of Victorian romance literature.

Marlene Springer says "Jude's soul loses control to Sue's psychosis" (Springer, 149), and by psychosis I think she means Sue's tendency to torture herself and others. D. H. Lawrence finds that "[i]t is quite natural that, with all her mental alertness, she married Phillotson without ever considering the physical quality of marriage. Deep instinct made her avoid the consideration. And the duality of her nature made her extremely liable to self-destruction. The suppressed, atrophied female in her, like a potent fury, was always there, suggesting to her to make the fatal mistake" (*Phoenix*, 497). She is blind to her motives and death-driven, Lawrence says, because she is dimly aware of how unhappy she is. She is a manipulator, taking revenge on the male who, over the centuries, has betrayed the female.[12]

Arabella's reentry into the story is accompanied by a dramatic shift in narrative tone. After Sue's marriage, Jude is at loose ends, too heartsick to stay in Melchester, too depressed to work in Christminster.

The very sight of the university is unbearable. At this point Arabella appears. Jude responds to her directness and down-to-earthness, but he does not permit himself to enjoy her company. He feels degraded by her, as if the obstacles to the high aim of his soul were entwined with Arabella's fleshy desires. Hardy endorses the disgust Jude feels for himself after sleeping with her and sympathizes with Jude's delight when he comes upon Sue, "so ethereal a creature that her spirit could be seen trembling through her limbs" (3:9). As Jude walks with her to Marygreen, it was "as if he carried a bright light."

Hardy employs the vulgarizing of Arabella as an artistic strategy by which he restores our sympathy for Jude's love of Sue. A. Alvarez marvels at Hardy's sleight of hand, "[at] the way in which Hardy managed to present the full, bitter sterility of [Sue's] narcissism and yet tried to exonerate her" (Alvarez, 118). The delicacy of Jude's love, their exquisite tuning in to one another—"Jude knew the quality of every vibration in Sue's voice, could read every symptom of her mental condition" (3:9)—affects our sympathy, so that when Jude attacks the institution of marriage even the nineteenth-century reader must have rooted for their happiness. Even their crabby Aunt Drusilla says there is something about Phillotson "that no woman of any niceness can stomach."

Hardy emphasized in his two letters to Gosse in November 1895 that *Jude* is constructed on contrasts "between the ideal life a man wished to lead, & the squalid real life he was fated to lead" (*Letters* II, 93). As Millgate (1971) points out, the very rhythm of the novel reflects the idea that the steadily downward curve of Jude's life, broken by alternate moments of doubt, fear, and hope, and finally shattering defeat, is meant to affect the reader with the sense of the hollowness of existence (in Bloom, 8). This tone of disillusionment is sounded in the parable with which Hardy concludes Part Third. Jude spends the whole of a Sunday, journeying like a pilgrim to a holy shrine, to meet the composer of a beautiful hymn called "The Foot of the Cross." The man has no sensitivity, however, nothing to offer Jude's troubled conscience but a list of commercial wines he is trying to market. The parable is a microcosm of the novel: Jude is spiritually excited, tries to anchor his feelings in concrete reality, and becomes disillusioned. The jewel in the casket always turns out to be a fake. The parable also suggests Jude's growing impatience with faith; the discrepancy between the lovely music and the mercantile composer represents the discrepancy between the ideal and the real, between Christ and Church.

PART FOURTH "AT SHASTON": QUIXOTIC FOLLIES

Much of Part Fourth suggests why Hardy originally titled his novel "The Simpletons." While he directs his farce and irony at Jude's and Sue's idealism and exposes the absurdity of living strictly by society's marital prescriptions, Hardy's feelings for Sue are divided between aversion for her narcissism and sympathy for it.

Kafka's aphorism "a cage went in search of a bird"[13] seems a fitting epigraph for Sue, whose married residence is a symbolic aerie, a cliff town where the new town rises out of the decay of what had been a citadel of medieval faith. She complains to Jude that she feels "crushed into the earth" (4:1) by the age of her old house and by the weight of generations of tradition.

When Jude calls Sue a flirt, the passion in his nature overrides his tact, and he presses an intimacy that strains their delicate reciprocity of feeling. She is forced to defend herself, but she wants at the same time to reestablish their spiritual harmony. After Jude has left, she calls to him from the window, expressing her thanks for his visit and her apologies for being difficult. For when "the high window-sill was between them, so that he could not get at her, she seemed not to mind indulging in a frankness she had feared at close quarters" (4:1).

Sue next meets Jude at their Aunt Drusilla's funeral, and she confesses that she has a physical revulsion against sex with her husband, "a personal feeling against it—a physical objection—a fastidiousness, or whatever it may be called" (4:2). Jude then seizes the opportunity and tells her (untruthfully) that he is involved with Arab-

"SHE LOOKED INTO HIS EYES WITH HER OWN TEARFUL ONES"

ella again. Sue reacts by "winc[ing] at the hit" and "look[ing] at the window pots with the geraniums and cactuses, withered for want of attention."

That night the sound of a rabbit writhing in a steel trap brings them together. In the immediate context the trapped rabbit is a symbol of Jude's coercive passion; more broadly it symbolizes the snares destined to mangle Jude's and Sue's happiness. He declares his love for her but she does not love him that way because she cannot. "So few could enter into my feeling—they would say 'twas my fanciful fastidiousness, or something of that sort" (4:2).

Yet the next morning when Sue is returning to Phillotson, Sue and Jude kiss "close and long" (4:3), and Jude realizes that he lives solely in the hope of possessing his married cousin. Shamed by the inconsistency of a "professor of the accepted school of morals" persisting "with headlong force in impassioned and illicit intentions," he resolves to abandon theology. He will not be a hypocrite. Hardy treats this minicrisis, this "turning point" in the life of his hero, with characteristic farce. Jude muses, "Strange that his first aspiration—towards academical proficiency—had been checked by a woman, and that his second aspiration—towards apostleship—had also been checked by a woman. 'Is it', he said, 'that the women are to blame; or is it the artificial system of things, under which the normal sex-impulses are turned into devilish domestic gins and springes to noose and hold back those who want to progress?' "

Jude's meditation on his situation is funny. Is his life messed up because of women, or does the political and cultural system prevent him from having both love and a bishopric? Hardy caricatures his hero as a lusty devil with a three-pronged pitchfork, burning books in an attempt to diminish his sense of guilt over pursuing a married woman. The flame in which Jude's theological and ethical works are consumed lights up the pigsty and his face, exaggerating the folly of his animal passion. The satire concludes with Jude breathing more freely, rid of his hypocritical encumbrances.

Balancing the section in which Jude burns his books is the section in which Sue breaks her marriage contract with Phillotson. To Phillotson's reproach that she is behaving monstrously in requesting that they live apart, she answers as Jude had answered Farmer Troutham after the farmer had walloped him. She tells Phillotson that the universe is to blame for her aversion to him: "things in general [are to blame] because they are so horrid and cruel!" (4:3). Sue is crying for the tomboy days of her childhood, for the garden of love that has been irrevocably spoiled by priests and husbands. She implores Phillotson to let her live with Jude, appealing to his generosity and strength of character and seizing upon all arguments, including a rousing passage from John Stuart Mill with which she exhorts Phillotson not to be an apish slave to convention and at least let her live apart from him in the house. Like the poor rabbit writhing to be free, she is so frantic with terror and repugnance toward her husband's sexuality that when he enters her room one evening by mistake, she jumps from a bedroom window.

"[A]nd this being the case," Phillotson tells his friend Gillingham, "I have come to a conclusion: that it is wrong to so torture a fellow-creature any longer" (4:4). Generous, even gallant, Phillotson finds

Sue and Jude's love for each other "not an ignoble, merely animal, feeling," but a unique and beautiful "affinity"; he characterizes their love as Shelleyan. "They seem to be one person split in two!" he declares. "The more I reflect, the more *entirely* I am on their side!"

Lawrence attempts to divine Hardy's motives, believing Hardy has only a dim awareness of his deepest attitudes to his characters. Yet his art tells the truth, Lawrence says. "She asked for what [Jude] could not give—what perhaps no man can give: passionate love without physical desire" (*Phoenix*, 509). Jude is drawn to her because "the whole human effort, towards pure life in the spirit, towards becoming pure Sue, drags him along" (*Phoenix*, 509). What Phillotson refers to as Shelleyan—the couple's marvelous reciprocity of feeling sans sex— Hardy, Lawrence says, felt as a sickness. Although Hardy's prejudice against the flesh is contradicted by the sensuousness of his language, it is exposed by the pessimism of his vision. All of Hardy's great novels, Lawrence says, tell the same tragic story of how people have violated their sensuous beings and won emotional paralysis as a result. Lawrence feels justified in "correcting" Hardy's art by showing what he thought Hardy meant: Jude's love for Sue is a dire warning of civilization's approaching terminal illness. The real tragedy, the danger that Jude is also bodiless and will accept Sue's bodiless love, is averted by Arabella, who in effect saves his soul. Though Jude and Sue are destroyed by Jude's passion, death is better than the gruesome spiritual leprosy of mental love. The elements of parody and farce in the novel reveal the extent of Hardy's self-awareness. His grin is self-derisive. That the novel is a pastiche of parody and ambiguities proves that Hardy writes with full consciousness, and that Sue, like everything else in the narrative, is both exposed to ridicule and reclaimed for admiration.

Sue elopes with Jude, saying, "I fear I am doing you a lot of harm. Ruining your prospects of the Church; ruining your progress in your trade; everything" (4:5). She wants emotional intimacy but seems terrified of passion, lest it destroy her. "My liking for you is not as some women's perhaps. But it is a delight in being with you, of a supremely delicate kind, and I don't want to go further." Jude realizes that he is in psychic danger, but he is susceptible to her wish that he not pester her by asking for more kisses like "a greedy boy"—probably the exact words she used in putting off her Christminster graduate.

Although Sue appears to be disembodied and aerial, she is not above jealousy. She weeps and rails at Jude when she learns that he had slept in the same Aldbrickham inn with Arabella. At this point he enters into a description of the spirit of Sue's love-making: "[W]hen I put my arms round you I almost expect them to pass through you as through air! Forgive me for being gross" (4.5).

Now that she is in control of their relationship, she feels safe.

> "Say those pretty lines, then, from Shelley's 'Epipsychidion' as if they meant me! . . . These are some of them:
> 'There was a Being whom my spirit oft
> Met on its visioned wanderings far aloft.
>
> . . . .
>
> A seraph of Heaven, too gentle to be human,
> Veiling beneath that radiant form of woman . . .'
> O it is too flattering, so I won't go on! But say it's me!—say it's me!"
> "It *is* you, dear; exactly like you!"
> "Now I forgive you! And you shall kiss me just once there— not very long."

In some ways chapter 5 of Part Fourth is the essence of ambiguity. Is Hardy admiring Sue's delicacy and Jude's sensitivity, or is he laughing at her prudery and his fear of sex? The tongue-in-cheek tone seems very strong, and surely the punch line, "there—not very long" is both a criticism of Sue and a parody of Victorian romance.

John Fowles says that for every writer the artistic process itself is a "doomed and illicit hunt" to recover the magic of childhood, and that Sue is Hardy's/Jude's illicit obsession, an erotically elusive incarnation of the unattainable mother.[14] He suspects that Hardy finds "his deepest pleasure in the period when consummation remains a distant threat," and that "the tryst is not the embodiment of a transient hope in the outward narrative so much as a straight desire for transience"

(Fowles 36–37). Thus, Jude and Sue read "Epipsychidion" instead of making love. Thus, too, there is mockery in Hardy's portrayal.

Patricia Ingham argues that Sue is different from the women in Hardy's other novels: Sue is "identifiable as a New Woman, by her explicit awareness of herself as a member of an oppressed sex rightly seeking autonomy."[15] With Sue, Ingham says, Hardy has created a woman who sees her "rights" in terms of existential choices. Her assertion of personal autonomy "depends on her assumption that it overrides other claims, including the traditional ones of husband, children and society" (Ingham 1989, 94). This is why, when Sue is breaking free from her husband, she claims the right to remain unmarried and sexually uncommitted to Jude. According to Ingham, by attaching these claims to the same man Hardy captures the contradictions of the nineteenth-century woman's position most forcibly and creates ambivalence as to whether Sue desires Jude (Ingham 1985, xix).

In discussing *Jude* in the context of Hardy's fiction as a whole, Ingham observes that over the course of his novel writing his treatment of women diverges from the cultural stereotype of female renunciation. Because Victorian women were not only dependent but ready to cultivate and display that dependence, a husband was their only goal and reward. Herbert Spencer justified traditional misogyny "scientifically" in his popular *The Study of Sociology* (1873) by claiming that women had less power for abstract reasoning because their vital energies were rerouted to nurturing offspring. As a result, they lagged behind men in the evolutionary process, having smaller brains as well as weaker physiques. As the weaker sex, Spencer argued, women had learned to disguise their feelings, to please and persuade, and to delight in submission, and women had developed an extra capacity for awe, which was why they were more religious than men.

Ingham observes that Hardy breaks with this stereotype and permits his fictional women their own moments of autonomous inner life. The break widens, she says, when Hardy consciously makes women a metaphor for workingmen. Women are victimized through sex and suffer, like workingmen, from self-devaluation and humiliating inferiority. Obviously permitting women autonomy radically subverts the

Christian ideal that a woman's self-fulfillment is rooted in self-denial. Thus Sue and Jude spring into life as twins who suffer a similar oppression. "They have other affinities," Ingham says, "but this goes deepest and is the reason why their claims to two-in-oneness are not absurd" (Ingham 1985, xviii).

Ingham considers *Jude* the "most feminist of all Victorian novels" because of Sue's autonomy and because the stereotypical "fallen," or defective, woman, the most depraved of all sinners, refuses to fall (Ingham 1985, xix). The fallen Arabella is at ease with her sexuality; she is candid, aggressive, and guilt-free. Hardy not only subverts the fallen woman story but also treats marriage as farce: Arabella marries Jude twice, commits bigamy with Bartlett, marries Bartlett, and is on a path to a fifth marriage with Vilbert at the novel's close; Sue and Jude find a period of happiness between their double marriages to the same partners.

That the collapse of Sue's autonomy is presented as inevitable and disastrous, Ingham says, is a uniquely feminist perspective for the time.

PART FIFTH "AT ALDBRICKHAM AND ELSEWHERE": DOWN, WANTONS

Jude the Obscure is the most farcically tragic of all of Hardy's novels. In it the small optimistic hopes end in small catastrophes, and the larger plot leads inexorably to one vast catastrophe. Each of the novel's six parts begins with hope and ends in despair, like an hourglass constantly being turned around, filling and being drained. The book's irony rests in its innocent beginnings. The hero is a sweet, generous person, patient and sincere, who breasts forward against the prejudice of his age and solicits his own destruction, in the process experiencing tragic illumination.

Some months have elapsed, and Jude and Sue share a little house, which Jude has furnished with his deceased aunt's belongings. He takes jobs lettering headstones, menial work by comparison to his labors as a cathedral mason, but he readily makes the sacrifice so that Sue can assist him with the lettering and not feel dependent. Both Sue and Jude have obtained divorces and are free to remarry, but Sue does not want to be married because a marriage contract would provide Jude with the additional pressure of a social claim on her body. His insistence brings out all her fears—of the Fawley curse, of the marriage contract, and of sexual hypocrisy.

Sue is content to live with Jude as a lover "only meeting by day" because he satisfies her desires to the letter. The fact that she refuses to sleep with him does not weaken our sympathy for her. But when Arabella comes knocking, Sue behaves too vulgarly for a seraph from heaven. Given Sue's aversion to sexual love, her crude display of jealousy is not merely an inconsistency but a form of despotism. Sue pleads with Jude that he not go to Arabella, contending that Arabella is no longer Jude's wife, so he has no further responsibilities to her. Jude, all too aware of the irony of Sue's argument, retorts, "And you are not either, dear, yet. . . . I've wanted you to be, and I've waited with the patience of Job, and I don't see that I've got anything by my self-denial" (5:2). Jude exhibits strength of character, one might say, in refusing to be brow-beaten. Sue then tries to prevent him from leaving the house by appealing to his nobler instincts, claiming that Arabella is low and coarse. He replies, "Perhaps I am coarse too, worse luck! I have the germs of every human infirmity in me, I verily believe—that was why I saw it was so preposterous of me to think of being a curate." The word "preposterous" drives home the threat that Jude's coarse flesh may meet other coarse flesh. "I do love you, Sue, though I have danced attendance on you so long for such poor returns! All that's best and noblest in me loves you, and your freedom from everything that's gross has elevated me, and enabled me to do what I should never have dreamt myself capable of, or any man, a year or two ago." With this bitterly ambiguous speech, thanking her for teaching him self-mastery, he turns to leave. At this point Sue caves in. "I agree," she cries, restraining him. "Only I didn't mean to! And I didn't want to marry again, either! . . . But, yes—I agree, I agree! I do love you."

Sue has responded to Jude's coercion, yet her jealous fears are well founded. Arabella, expecting Jude when Sue visits her hotel room the next morning, is lying in bed in a nightgown making dimples. Thus, the scenerio Sue had feared—talk, drink, seduction—which will

"THERE ON THE GRAVEL LAY A WHITE HEAP"

actually occur three years later, is credible. "Perhaps I should quite
have done it if it hadn't been for you," Arabella says, laughing. "Never
such a tender fool as Jude is if a woman seems in trouble, and coaxes
him a bit." (5:2).

Thus the narrative point of view is always shifting. The morning-
after scene, which we expect to be revealing, is remarkably neutral. It
begins cryptically: "The next morning it was wet" (5:2). Jude speaks
gaily; Sue has a glow. But she also smiles ruefully, telling him, "[t]he
little bird is caught at last!" The narrative relates nothing significant
about their feelings, and it is surprising, almost startling, that Sue
appears so content with the new arrangement, although Jude and Sue
still live in separate rooms. Indeed, there is no indication at this point
that they are either unhappy or deceiving themselves or incapable of
living in reality. Yet Hardy makes much of their reluctance to marry,
particularly Sue's; it dominates the foreground of several chapters, and
Hardy possibly depicts their vacillations in order to reveal their more
private feelings. Sue's antipathy to marriage must be powerful indeed

to overrule the practical wisdom of wedlock after the couple has adopted little Father Time. One suspects that her arguments are really aimed at protecting herself from Jude's possessiveness. Hardy admits as much in a letter of 20 November 1895: "one of her reasons for fearing the marriage ceremony is that she fears it wd be breaking faith with Jude to withhold herself at pleasure, or altogether, after it; though while uncontracted she feels at liberty to yield herself as seldom as she chooses." This presumably is why they maintain separate rooms after becoming lovers. "[H]er intimacies with Jude," Hardy writes in the same letter, "have never been more than occasional," and "[t]his has tended to keep his passion as hot at the end as at the beginning, & helps to break his heart. He has never really possessed her as freely as he desired" (*Letters* 2, 99).

Yet if Hardy had wanted to suggest that Sue's disgust for sex is what makes her reluctant to marry Jude, he blurs his intention by emphasizing the Fawley curse—a family proclivity for suicide and insanity going back through both sets of parents to legendary ancestors. Can Hardy mean, as J. I. M. Stewart has suggested, that there is a biological imperative in the Fawley blood that prompts Jude and Sue "to elect frustration and self-destruction?" Stewart maintains that "this [family trait] is what unites them, and at the same time confines them in an inalienable loneliness" (Stewart, 201)—as if they find their neuroses mutually compatible. Although this psychological fatalism undermines the radical social significance and tragic impact of the novel, there is truth in the observation that Jude and Sue have compatible neuroses. Jude is not as self-enclosed by the nervous intellectuality and fastidiousness that underlie Sue's criticisms of marriage, but he shares her feeling when she says that "[i]n fifty, a hundred, years" people will be so disgusted by themselves and their fellow creatures, "weltering humanity," that if they do marry, they will be afraid to reproduce themselves (5:4).

Jude and Sue appear perfectly happy at the agricultural show, that remarkable receptivity of feeling delighting them as if they were "the two parts of a single whole" (5:5). Sue appears as vividly in love as Jude: at the flower pavilion she declares, "I feel that we have returned to Greek joyousness, and have blinded ourselves to sickness and sorrow, and have forgotten what twenty-five centuries have taught the race since their time, as one of your Christminster luminaries says."

But the subtleties of chapter five imply that the lovers are cheating time, or possibly that such happiness can exist only out of time. It is telling that Hardy situates the fair at a point on the Great Western Highway where the road divides, meeting again many miles to the west. The town is a mixture of old and new, modern railway and ancient crumbling walls, a place where the future meets the past. The fair contains every kind of temporary structure. Hardy conveys the sense of a moment in isolation, a fleeting hour in June among the roses. Vilbert is present as well as little Father Time, for this is a still point between time past and time future, between the old dispensation's charlatan physician selling "immunity from the ravages of Time" (5:5) and the startled herald of time's sinister meaninglessness. Arabella spies on Jude and Sue from behind a beaded veil and buys from Vilbert a love potion made from the hearts of doves. Meanwhile Father Time tries not to see the withered roses. In this way Hardy lets us know that time past will betray, and time future will destroy. There is also a disturbing suggestion that the lovers are cheating time by refusing to get married. Hardy says, ironically, that although the boy aroused their concern for the future, they "tried to dismiss, for a while at least, a too strenuously forward view."

The strange boy has multiple meanings, depending on different ways of understanding Jude's character and dilemmas. On the level of a moral struggle, in which Jude the hero grapples with convention, Father Time highlights both the folly and the heroism of Jude's efforts. From Ian Gregor's perspective, Jude is naïve or weak, so little Time's "sorrowful contemplative eyes become ours as we watch [Jude and Sue] desperately attempting to cheat time, repudiating the past, evading the social commitments of the present, indifferent, with their ever-increasing family, to the demands of the future."[16] According to Terry Eagleton, Jude is courageous; consequently Father Time highlights Jude's struggle against his condition, as well as his tragic susceptibility to "the deathly ideology" of his society (Eagleton, 70).

A Reading of the Text

Society begins to drive a wedge between Jude and Sue. The neighbors conclude that their alliance must be sinful because they are happy. Little Father Time is called a bastard at school. Sue's "dull, cowed, and listless manner for days" (5:6) ought to have convinced Spring Street that the couple has married, but the neighbors remain hostile, because Jude and Sue cannot simulate the married state.

As Jude's business falls off adversity makes Sue superstitious about signs from heaven. As long as things go well her conscience is lenient, but when misfortune comes, she tends to interpret it as punishment—even God's punishment. The news that they must leave Aldbrickham shocks her and affects her morbidly. She appears to withdraw her physical love; she becomes brittle and pleads with Jude not to separate her from little Father Time, although such an act is inconceivable. Entreating on the boy's behalf is a kind of silent prayer, a suing for grace for herself.

A greater shock comes when Jude and Sue are dismissed from restoration work in the little church. The sight of an unwed woman and her lover refurbishing the letters of the law scandalizes the good dames of the parish. Although the community's point of view has some validity, Hardy's pained sympathy goes out powerfully to his hero and heroine. Yet society will win, and the auctioning of the couple's goods symbolically prophesies the death of their love. Sue's pet doves are sold to a poulterer. Later she liberates them from their cages, and the reader suspects that they will fly to Vilbert's dovecot where their hearts will be boiled down into love potions.

Society's pressure creates a rift in the lovers' sensibilities. While Sue becomes dependent and clinging, Jude develops an intellectual poise and dignity. While she begins to cringe before convention, he begins to defy it—by accepting with great self-possession his dismissal from the church and the workingman's improvement society. Ironically, the two are changing stances: Jude is progressing to a loss of faith, Sue to a "morbid religiosity"; time and adversity are enlarging his views and narrowing hers (Stewart, 193).

With the last scenes of Part Fifth, Hardy dramatizes a question: What does a just and moral man hold out for if "[c]ruelty is the law pervading all nature and society" (5:8)? After two and a half years as a wandering stonemason, Jude has been further reduced—by a serious illness—to baking gingerbread cakes, which Sue and little Time sell at a local fair. Their one friend in the world, Mrs. Edlin, looks after the convalescing man and tends the couple's two young children.

In mentioning her unborn child to Arabella, Sue bursts into tears: "But it seems such a terribly tragic thing to bring beings into the world—so presumptuous—that I question my right to do it sometimes!" (5:7)—presumptuous, that is, to inflict upon children the necessity of enduring life. There is bitter irony in the cakes they sell: Jude has molded them into tracery windows and cloisters of the colleges. Although he has lost his faith, "hardly a shred" of his old beliefs remaining, he cannot stop loving the institution. Sue laments that he remains blind to the reality of Christminster, "a nest of commonplace schoolmasters whose characteristic is timid obsequiousness to tradition," and that despite Jude's being denied and rejected, driven back "to zero, with all its humiliations" (5:8), he still dotes on the old dream.

Overall, it is ironic that Sue, whose spirit is crouching in extreme anxiety for a decisive sign from heaven, complains of "timid obsequiousness"; that Arabella, the scheming realist, preaches spiritual resignation; and that Jude, the nonbeliever, burns with the fever of a born evangelist, while Sue, the penitent, trembling on the verge of conversion, quenches his fire.

The irony of *Jude*, in part, derives from Hardy's reaction to his lifelong fascination with Shelley, who expresses the unsustainable part of Hardy's temperament. In Shelley's work, people are still capable of making their dreams come true. "To love, and bear; to hope, till Hope creates / From its own wreck the thing it contemplates," is the way of renewal proclaimed in the final speech of Shelley's *Prometheus Unbound*.[17] For Shelley hope is a duty, allied with a passionate belief in life; for Hardy, life punishes dreamers. Hope begets not the thing it contemplates but a slow suicide: hope bleeds Jude white.

Hardy's love for Shelley's marvelous visionary energy, set off against his own ineffectual flapping against the strictures of convention, surely contributes to the restless mood swings of the novel. Jude and Sue are occasionally the butts of farce, but they are never pathetic; in the battle between illusion and reality their dreams make a powerful spiritual claim, revealing a thirst for beauty and fulfillment, a thirst that makes them rebellious, giving them the strength to live and, in the end, to destroy themselves.

Do not sprout wings of the spirit too much, Hardy warns; hope can only kill you. The rhythm of the novel reinforces this idea; each of its six parts is an hourglass constantly turning upside down with hope and emptying into despair. There is a renewed high purpose at the start of each part and, at the end, a corresponding decay: Part First begins with a sense of mission and ends with a suicide attempt; the second part begins with new purpose at Christminster and ends in defeat at Marygreen; Part Third begins with hope for Sue and ends in desolation after her marriage to Phillotson; the fourth part begins with a passionate, mutual handclasp and ends with the equivocal success of a sexless union; Part Fifth begins with a happy union and ends in beggary, and the last part begins in a spirit of bleak hope and ends with a denial of life.

PART SIXTH "AT CHRISTMINSTER AGAIN": NEVER SUCH INNOCENCE AGAIN

Jude chooses to reenter Christminster on Remembrance Day, the university's day of commemoration and commencements, when the populace throngs the main streets to cheer the sons of the university. "Humiliation Day for me!" he says to Sue, who later refers to the city as Jerusalem and explicitly identifies Jude with Christ when she says, "[l]eaving Kennetbridge for this place is like coming from Caiaphas to Pilate!" (6:1). Jude steps forth to address the populace. Following the example of Christ's criticism of the temple, he criticizes the frieze on a college building, then turns to the issue exemplified by his life. Can it be wrong to follow the bent of one's nature and attempt to cross social barriers? Because he is always on the verge of self-recrimination, as if the germ of failure lay in him, the edge of his bitterness cuts in several directions. Perhaps, he says, he is a victim of the mental and social restlessness of the time. His words imply that he is an object lesson. But what sort of lesson? That struggling against class and convention is worthless? He perceives that something is wrong with the social formulas; his own worn-out life and the failure and despair of workingmen like him cry out for social change. The people cheer him, and his old compatriot Tinker Taylor remarks, "And this only a working man!"

An ugly spectacle takes place in front of the crowd. A cabman, having failed to deliver a gowned doctor right to his door on schedule, kicks his horse in exasperation. The rich man rushing off in his robes and leaving the cabman, robbed of his tip, to take it out on his horse, illustrates the cruelty of the pecking order—the indignity paid to those at the bottom and the indifference of society. It is a performance made to order for Jude. Jude is warned to keep his place by a policeman, but soon he is gripped again with fervent admiration for Christminster. His wife and children wait with unnatural patience in the rain, while Jude strains to hear the speeches in Latin, catching an occasional "*um* or *ibus*" from an open window, until a renewal of bitterness breaks his trance and he apologizes to Sue for indulging his infatuation.

R. P. Draper says of Jude's return to Christminster, "If he is not quite the proverbial dog needlessly returning to his own vomit, he is rather like the venturer on a second marriage whose action, according to Dr. Johnson, represents 'the triumph of hope over experience.' "[18] Philip Weinstein takes it a step further, contending that there is nothing ennobling in Jude's speech to the crowd. It is absurd posturing, play-acting. Jude simply cannot face himself as an ordinary man; he cannot look about him and chart the most intelligent course. "[I]nstead" according to Weinstein, "he leaps into the transcendent and allusive ideal" (Weinstein 132–33). This view of Jude's idealism as an addiction and an abdication is shared by Ian Gregor, who criticizes Jude's naïve, pretentious attitude toward a society that is immune "to prophesy and to judgment" (Gregor, 242).

Perhaps, however, Hardy intends no mockery in the street scene

"'I OUGHT NOT TO BE BORN, OUGHT I?'"

but rather has a straightforward intention. Terry Eagleton says Jude has learned to disentangle himself from delusion, and his return to Christminster shows him refusing "to back down from the question of his own identity" (Eagleton, 66). For Eagleton, Jude is "a genuinely tragic protagonist because the value released in [his] defeat, the insistence on a recognition of his total humanity, challenges" the oppressive forces of convention (Eagleton, 66).

Jude's increasing alienation from Sue is conveyed by his blindness to her nervousness, her growing susceptibility to premonitions and signs, and her nearness to collapse. Her shock at seeing Phillotson in the crowd, a premonition of her devastating reversal, sounds the mournful tones of the future: "I felt a curious dread of him; an awe, or terror, of conventions I don't believe in. It comes over me at times like a sort of creeping paralysis" (6:1). The stresses of concealing her pregnancy and confronting one hostile landlady after another are unbearable shocks to Sue's nervous system. After confessing to the woman who has taken her in for the night that she is not married, Sue lapses into a quiet reverie and watches the rain; it is a moment of suspension from all pressure, a moment of absolute resignation.

The maudlin and highly exaggerated deaths of all her children is the event that finally breaks Sue. The social context of the tragedy that is about to occur is expressed by Hardy's setting the grotesque scene in the shadow of the outer walls of Sarcophagus College, its "four centuries of gloom, bigotry, and decay" darkening the room (6:2). In a deeply anxious mood after her failure to acquire lodgings for the next day, Sue blurts out to Father Time, "[a]ll is trouble, adversity and suffering!" (6:2). Society, not an angry Providence, has uprooted the family and turned it from lodging houses. Sue, too weak to bear this burden any longer, unloads her troubles on one far too young to bear them, and Father Time assumes the symbolic role of nemesis. He expresses her feelings: "It would be better to be out o' the world than in it, wouldn't it? . . . But we don't ask to be born? . . . I think that whenever children be born that are not wanted they should be killed directly, before their souls come to 'em, and not allowed to grow big and walk about!"

A Reading of the Text

At Kennetbridge Fair, Sue had cried to Arabella that it was presumptuous to bring children into the world. When Sue tells Father Time there will soon be another child, he echoes her earlier sentiment by crying, "How *ever* could you, mother, be so wicked and cruel!" (6:2). In Freudian terms, Father Time is that "portion of the ego, which sets itself over against the rest of the ego as super-ego, and which now, in the form of 'conscience' " punishes the ego for its sinfulness.[19] Sue begs the boy to forgive her, both of them crying, but his reproaches are bitter: "I won't forgive you, ever, ever!" When he says what she is thinking, that if the children were all dead there would be no trouble at all, she answers, "peremptorily," that he should not think that, and he should go to sleep.

D. H. Lawrence says that Father Time acts out what Sue really feels: that she should not have had children, and that Father Time is an anachronism, an accident, unreal, and is not meant to live (*Phoenix*, 508). Perhaps Sue's antipathy to motherhood, her revulsion against adulthood, is why Hardy never gives her young children an existence in the novel. They make no sounds: they are sacks in their parents' arms.

After the murders and suicide, Hardy eulogizes little Father Time from Sue's point of view: "[o]n that little shape had converged all the inauspiciousness and shadow which had darkened the first union of Jude, and all the accidents, mistakes, fears, errors of the last. . . . For the rashness of those parents he had groaned, for their ill-assortment he had quaked, and for the misfortunes of these he had died" (6:2). Jude breaks down like Sue, but he does not condemn himself. He does not feel like "a spectacle unto the world"; he does not see an angry Providence in the face of the dead boy. Not feeling Sue's guilt and need for punishment, Jude fails to understand that her morbidity is rooted in a terror of God.

When Sue's "intellect scintillated like a star" (6:3), she was an atheist, cynically speculating that if there were a Supreme Intelligence, he had not calculated the evolution of the human faculty and its susceptibility to suffering. But guilt, making her "more bodeful of the direct antagonism of things," converts these speculations into a religious angst, a fear that she and Jude are being persecuted for their sins. "We must conform!" she exclaims. "All the ancient wrath of the Power above us has been vented upon us, His poor creatures, and we must submit. There is no choice. We must. It is no use fighting against God!" Their differences cannot be reconciled. Sue argues that one must earn forgiveness from God; Jude argues that one must fight "only against man and senseless circumstance."

Hardy has an eye on book 10 of Milton's *Paradise Lost*, where Adam and Eve appraise the catastrophe of having eaten the apple. Sue, like Adam and Eve, seeks God's forgiveness: "He will instruct us praying"—but Jude does not. Jude feels only a lover's guilt for having caused his beloved pain, for having imposed his will and made her his mistress. Sue, desperate to attach a religious significance to her guilt that she may relieve it, insists that he was not the seducer; it had been, rather, the daring of their intellect—"a dreadful sense of my own insolence of action" (6:3)—that must be quelled and paid for: "I have thought that we have been selfish, careless, even impious, in our courses, you and I. Our life has been a vain attempt at self-delight. But self-abnegation is the higher road. . . . I should like to prick myself all over with pins and bleed out the badness that's in me!" Jude tries to shake sense into her: "That a woman-poet, a woman-seer, a woman whose soul shone like a diamond—whom all the wise of the world would have been proud of, if they could have known you—should degrade herself like this! I am glad I had nothing to do with Divinity—damn glad—if it's going to ruin you in this way!"

He almost accuses her of betrayal, but he suppresses the full force of his vehemence. Instead of accusing her of selfishness, he blames the female sex for lacking reason and implores her not to sacrifice their love. He borrows her tone of resignation, and for several moments they review the past from her perspective of sin. "We ought to have lived in mental communion, and no more," she says (6:3). She admits that she acquiesed out of fear that he would go back to Arabella, and although she came to love him, her love was tainted at its source, a "selfish and cruel wish to make your heart ache for me without letting mine ache for you."

A Reading of the Text

Lawrence believes that Christianity has betrayed them both. He rejects the idea that there was any happiness between them; there was only what he calls an "unhealthy condition of lightened consciousness," which is why, at the agricultural fair, the roses had "more being than either he or she" (*Phoenix*, 506). His point is that Jude becomes exhausted, aimless, and pathetically nonproductive because of the bodilessness of Sue's love, and that by the time of Part Sixth, her death-dealing Christianity has made him moribund. To Lawrence, the death of the children accelerates the grotesque influence of centuries of ultra-Christianity. Sue's "loathed" body must be "scourged out of existence" with the deaths; nothing should remain but the will by which she annihilates herself. She stamps out her mind, as one stamps out fire, in "the embracing of utter orthodoxy, where every belief, every thought, every decision was made ready for her, so that she did not exist self-responsible" (*Phoenix*, 509). Going back to Phillotson is the bitterest penance she can inflict upon herself; it is an act of pure "life-hatred."

A. Alvarez says that Sue ends as she began, "fixed in her narcissism," incapable of giving herself. He agrees with Lawrence that Jude and Sue were never happy, although until the closing scenes Jude manages to convince himself otherwise and makes Sue conform to his Shelleyan ideal by "a kind of emotional sleight of mind" (Alvarez, 119, 118). Her ruling passion has always been to preserve "her self-inclosed mould," and her recantation does just that. Alvarez says her self-abnegation protects her from the truth that she is the major destructive force in their relationship.

But in the scenes depicting her return to Phillotson, in chapters 4 and 5 of Part Sixth, Hardy is concerned with the external forces that crush independent thinking. Two intelligent individuals agree to a marriage in which the woman sacrifices the man she loves to give herself in corpselike submission to a man who knows she physically detests him. "[T]he world and its ways have a certain worth," Sue says when bidding farewell to Jude (6:4). This is a maxim that Phillotson has come round to also. Knocked about "from pillar to post" by the hands of the virtuous, Phillotson, too, recants, because he has learned to see his former generous conduct to her as "illogical disregard of opinion, and of the principles in which he had been trained." Ruin comes from flying in the teeth of social convention. Parts Fifth and Sixth, Ian Gregor says, "are there to show that 'the mere judgment of man' is for [Hardy] an inextricable part of man's soul" (Gregor, 238). "I was always against your opening the cage-door and letting the bird go in such an obviously suicidal way" says Phillotson's best man, Gillingham (6:5). This bloodless point of view runs as an undertow beneath Jude's anguished cry, "[e]rror—perversity! It drives me out of my senses. . . . It will be a fanatic prostitution" (6:4); beneath the chorus effect of Mrs. Edlin's heated opposition to the marriage; and beneath Hardy's satirical stabs at the Church for congratulating Phillotson on setting things right. Gillingham makes a second cynical observation, which reinforces the novel's sardonic undercurrent, that you cannot win no matter what you do. The best man looked at the happy groom "and wondered whether it would ever happen that the reactionary spirit induced by the world's sneers . . . would make Phillotson more orthodoxly cruel to her than he had erstwhile been informally and perversely kind." That Gillingham's prophesy will come to pass is evident in the way Phillotson behaves to Mrs. Edlin, whose opposition to his remarrying Sue makes him sadistic. "A great piece of laxity will be rectified," he declares. The irony is the letter of the law kills, but so does the spirit of the gospels: Phillotson has become a bully by following the example of Christ.

Sue pathetically preaches the spirit of the gospels to Jude when she is begging for his forgiveness. "Your generous devotion to me is unparalleled, Jude!" she says when they part. "Your worldly failure, if you have failed, is to your credit rather than to your blame. Remember that the best and greatest among mankind are those who do themselves no worldly good. . . . The devoted fail. . . . 'Charity seeketh not her own' " (6:4). There is a melancholy irony in Sue using the language of Christian charity to console Jude after she has betrayed him.

After the fair at Stout Newton, the chronicle of Jude's history is a free-fall into misfortune and calamity. His second marriage to Arabella reestablishes a tone of black comedy. Jude has gone back to zero—

the same woman, with the same strategy to seduce him; even the pig metaphor is the same—the couple takes a room above a pork and sausage shop. Jude is playacting, Philip Weinstein says, lost in a "proliferation of weightless abstract identities" (Weinstein, 133), and as oblivious to reality as ever. When entrapped by Arabella, he prates, quotes, delivers speeches with elaborate rhetorical figures, all of which are futile efforts to idealize himself. But the counterpoint is a narrative sympathy for Jude. His marriage to Arabella portrays the trajectory of his life: his future has turned into his past, and in moving forward he has regressed. In his despair we see the image of Father Time.

Little Father Time, with his octogenarian's face, is Jude's inner reality after Sue abandons him. The boy stands for the concentrated life experience of his father—that is, the young boy's fate is a prediction and fulfillment of the hero's defeat. Looking back, one sees the doom foretold in the resemblance between young Jude and his son. Jude's face as a boy bears the same fixity of thought, the same look of "an ancient man" (1:4). Many of the novel's early scenes symbolize the bitter disappointment to come. Jude stares into the village well— "a long circular perspective ending in a shining disk of quivering water" (1:1)—as he dreams of following Phillotson to Christminster. There is a morning fog; everything is misted over but the boy's inner eye on the shining orb of his dream, until his trance is broken by his aunt's shrill outcry, "idle young harlican!" (1:1). Reality pulls him up. Farmer Troutham smacks him on the buttocks and swings him about like "a hooked fish" for being too tenderhearted—for communing with aerial beings (1:2). Jude lies down on a heap of litter near a pigsty and peers at the sky through his straw hat, dimly understanding that he wants something to believe in. He does not want to be ordinary. Growing up frightens him. At the end he dies in a state of total nihilism. Just as his son dies by hanging, Jude dies out of his element like "a hooked fish."

But this fatalistic perspective—that calamity is the law of life—is balanced by Hardy's indignant and sustained attack on the oppressiveness of social convention. Jude adopts little Father Time before he is certain of his paternity. His idea that parents should not possess children is both a form of special pleading and an attack on the traditional idea of family. He says, "All the little ones of our time are collectively the children of us adults of the time, and entitled to our general care. That excessive regard of parents for their own children, and their dislike of other people's, is, like class-feeling, patriotism, save-your-own-soul-ism, and other virtues, a mean exclusiveness at bottom" (5:3). Jude does not want his child to grow up in a pothouse with a mother who does not want him. He does not want his son to die cursing the day he was born. But his charity backfires. Society turns against them, fails to give them room, and Jude's child and Jude himself die cursing the day they were born. Everything that Jude believes in— college, Church, social convention, and finally even Sue—pushes him down and wears him out.

Of all the forces that break Jude's will—fate, social prejudice, his own folly—the most crushing is the power of Christian Orthodoxy because it destroys Sue. The perspective in the final scenes comes from St. Paul: "[t]hough I give my body to be burned, and have not charity, it profiteth me nothing" (6:6). In her conversion to "true religion" (6:7), Sue martyrs herself, dutifully giving her body to Phillotson—a grotesque submission that earns her neither forgiveness nor peace. She prays for courage outside her husband's door, flees to her room when he does not answer, and confesses a hope that he may be dead before finally submitting her body.

Jude comes to see that the forms, conventions, and religious duties of society are unnatural, often immoral, even depraved, and that there is no meaning to human suffering. Hardy makes Jude the chorus to his own tragedy in Jude's speech to Mrs. Edlin about Sue:

> [S]he was once a woman whose intellect was to mine like a star to a benzoline lamp: who saw all *my* superstitions as cobwebs that she could brush away with a word. Then bitter affliction came to us, and her intellect broke, and she veered round to darkness. . . . [N]ow the ultimate horror has come—her giving herself like this to what she loathes, in her enslavement to forms! . . . [W]hen we were at our own best, long ago—when our minds were clear, and our love of truth fearless—the time was not ripe for us! Our ideas were fifty years too

soon to be any good to us. And so the resistance they met with brought
reaction in her, and recklessness and ruin on me! (6:10)

This choral statement concludes with Jude cursing convention and
blaspheming God. His reckless abandonment of life is the final act of
a tragedy—tragedy as defined by Schopenhauer in a sentence Hardy
copied into his notebook in the summer of 1891: "Only when intellect
rises to the point where the vanity of all effort is manifest, & the will
proceeds to an act of self-annulment, is the drama tragic in the true
sense" (quoted in Millgate 1982, 315).

Narrative indignation against society inflames the final scenes as
Hardy repeatedly hammers out the name Cardinal College. Jude is
stricken by the cold off the "meadows of Cardinal"—"death claws,"
Hardy calls the chill, the "freezing negative" Jude encounters at every
turn. At the moment of his death Arabella enters "the quad of
Cardinal," which workmen are decorating for a ball (6:11). She walks
down "Cardinal Street" to the river after finding him dead. Fashion-
able people are "pouring out of Cardinal meadow," and a waltz joy-
ously throbs from "the ball-room at Cardinal," while Jude lies dead
and covered with a sheet.

The hammering reiteration of the name "Cardinal" seems to point
up Jude's agony and death as a crucifixion. Like Jesus on the Cross,
the dying Jude with burning throat cries for water: " 'Sue—darling—
drop of water—please—O please!' No water came" (6:11). In Mark
(15:36) vinegar is the drink sponged on Jesus's lips in derision after
he cries, "My God, my God, why hast thou forsaken me?" Jude receives only mockery—shouts and hurrahs—vinegar mingled with gall.
Jude's death may also have reminded Hardy of Lazarus in the St. Luke
parable (16:19) of the rich man and the beggar who gets not even
crumbs from the rich man's table but dogs to lick his sores. These
allusions to Jesus questioning God and Lazarus covered with sores
culminate with the final image of Jude as Job.

Jude, heaped in misery, recites Job's lament (Job 3:3, 11, 20).
"Let the day perish wherein I was born. . . . Why died I not from the
womb? . . . Wherefore is light given to him that is in misery . . . ?"

(6:11). The bitterness of the closure edges on sardonic mockery. Vilbert of the dovecot and love potions is Jude's successor with Arabella. He smooches her and the old world triumphs. Meanwhile the crowd roars its hurrahs. Later organ notes and applause reach the dead man's room from an auditorium where honorary degrees are being conferred on the aristocracy. In the room with the corpse lie the few books with which he taught himself, "dog-eared" and "roughened with stone-dust." "All was still within. The bumping of near thirty years had ceased."

Christian medievalists thought of young Joseph, the dreamer, imprisoned by his brothers in a well, as a prefiguration of the betrayed Christ in his tomb, and these two iconographic symbols of betrayal frame the novel. It begins with Jude mourning his imprisonment in Marygreen while staring into the village well and ends with him lying in an open coffin, attended by Mrs. Edlin and Arabella. The two women, positioned on either side of their beloved Jude like the two Marys attending the corpse of Christ at the Entombment complete the allusion to Christ that is prefigured in the opening of the novel. But the meaning of the Entombment is reversed; there is no resurrection to come. The smile that flickers on Jude's face has a hint of mockery in it. The two Marys are earthy, sharp-eyed, and sharp-tongued. What they say about Sue—that she has not found peace and never will no matter how hard she prays—is irreverent and fatally true. The scene is an ironic distortion of a sacred image, Hardy's final indictment of Christianity for betraying Jude's and Sue's humanity.

THE EPIGRAPHS

Hardy uses the standard Victorian technique of the epigraph for each section of the book, adding all of them after he finished the manuscript. Most of them have a double meaning in their play upon the text—in the way they indicate multiple points of view. Hardy chose quotations that have ironically different meanings in their original context, as opposed to what they suggest out of context, so that conflicting authorial directives are given simultaneously.

The epigraph to the whole book is "the letter killeth," from 2 Corinthians 3:6: "For the letter killeth, but the spirit giveth life." The letter of the law is written "in tables of stone," but the spirit of God—charity—is written "in the fleshy tables of the heart" (2 Corinthians 3:3). Charity is Hardy's text and the incompleteness of the quotation is vital. The missing clause, "but the spirit giveth life," indicates that because society with its ordinances and prejudices lacks charity, individuals are destroyed.

Part First

The epigraph to "At Marygreen" stands both as a warning and a prediction: "Yea, many there be that have run out of their wits for women, and become servants for their sakes. Many also have perished, have erred, and sinned, for women. . . . O ye men, how can it be but women should be strong, seeing they do thus?" The quotation is taken from one of the books of the Apocrypha, I Esdras (4: 26–27, 32). Out of context, the passage points up the weakness of Jude—the folly of the flesh and its power over the spirit. Taken in context, the irony of the quote is double-edged, its barb aimed at society as well as Jude.

The first book of Esdras tells how Darius, King of Persia, is reneging on his promise to rebuild Jerusalem and the temple of the Jews. In the course of things he holds a contest to see who among his guards can produce the wisest sentence. One writes, "wine is the strongest"; the second, "the king is the strongest"; the third, Zorobabel, writes, "women are strongest: but above all things Truth beareth away the victory." As his prize for winning, Zorobabel insists that Darius fulfill his promise to the Jews.

Compared with its original context, the quotation points ahead to reversals and disappointments in Jude's career. Hardy's quotation is clipped short, omitting reference to the power of truth, because the truth—wisdom, the spirit of God—that inspires Zorobabel does not help Jude to fulfill his mission. Jude is destroyed by "wine," "the King," and "women"—that is, by his own folly, by a "Christian" society lacking truth and charity, and by Sue and Arabella.

Part Second

The two quotations introducing "At Christminster" warn against the disabling power of illusion. The first, from Swinburne, "Save his own soul he hath no star," is from line 15 of the "Prelude" to the collection *Songs Before Sunrise* (1871). The poem celebrates self-reliance. Lose yourself in the flux of passions and dreams, Swinburne says, but count them as things that pass. The individual must maintain his self-possession.

> Man's soul is man's god. . . .
> Save his own soul's light overhead
> None leads him and none ever led . . .
> Save his own soul he has no star
> And sinks unless his own soul guide
> Helmless in middle turn of tide.[20]

The epigraph in Hardy's context points to an opposite meaning: Jude founders because he steers his course by the stars of Christminster and Sue, stars outside himself, which dazzle him and prevent him from directing his own life.

The second epigraph—"*Notitiam primosque gradus vicinia fecit; tempore crevit amor*," "nearness led to awareness and the first steps: love grew with time"—is from Ovid's *Metamorphoses*, (4:59–60). Just as Ovid's work tells of Pyramus' love for Thisbe, with whom he can communicate only through a chink in the wall (4:55–172), so Jude peers through the walls of Christminster, denied entrance, and is shut out from Sue by the wall of her self-containment. Like Pyramus, he kills himself for love.

Part Third

"At Melchester" is headed by one line from Sappho: "For there was no other girl, O bridegroom, like her." Since most of Sappho's poetry has survived only as fragments or quotations, there is no complete context for this line. It seems to have come from Sappho's epithalamia, that is, her bridal songs. The irony in this section is that Sue is a bride who abhors marriage, dislikes erotic love, and is not marrying Jude, who is ironically referred to as "O bridegroom."

Hardy read H. T. Wharton's more or less literal translation of Sappho. The bridal fragments, numbered 91 to 117, include 96: "I shall be ever maiden"; 102: "Do I still long for maidenhood?"; 109: "Maidenhood, maidenhood, whither art thou gone away from me? Never again will I come to thee, never again"; 99: "Happy bridegroom, now is thy wedding come to thy desire, and thou hast the maiden of thy desire"; 106: "For there was no other girl, O bridegroom, like her."[21] In these fragments the bride is reluctant, like Sue, to forgo her innocence, while the bridegroom is on fire with desire. Part Third is largely a farce of such cross purposes. Is Hardy, by using Sappho, also implying sexual ambiguity?

Part Fourth

The epigraph to "At Shaston" is from the introduction to Milton's pamphlet *The Doctrine and Discipline of Divorce* (1644): "whoso prefers either Matrimony, or other Ordinance before the Good of Man and the plain Exigence of Charity, let him profess Papist, or Protestant, or what he will, he is no better than a Pharisee [and understands not the Gospel]."[22] Milton argues that divorce is preferable to a bad marriage and that to constrain people in a bad marriage violates the Gospel. So when Phillotson lets Sue go he is as forward-looking as Milton—a person of independent judgment and natural charity. But when he takes her back and becomes socially obedient, a good Christian, he is, in fact, a Pharisee.

Part Fifth

The epigraph to "At Aldbrickham and Elsewhere" is from the *Meditations* of Marcus Aurelius Antoninus (Roman emperor and philosopher, 121–180 AD) as translated by George Long.[23] The work is a spiritual diary that the emperor kept, in Greek, in the form of reflections addressed to himself and that he entitled "Eis Heauton," "To Himself." Hardy quotes from Book 11, paragraph 20: "Thy aerial part and all the fiery parts which are mingled in thee, though by nature they have an upward tendency, still in obedience to the disposition of the universe they are overpowered here in the compound mass [the body]." Out of context, this excerpt suggests the power of the flesh over the spirit. Accordingly, in Part Fifth, Jude, overcome by the flesh, coerces Sue to sleep with him; they adopt his child by Arabella, and Sue bears children. In context, the quotation suggests something else, namely, that Jude's spirit is rebellious and that he is responsible for his misfortunes. Marcus Aurelius says that although his other elements stay in place, his intelligent part, his spark of divine reason, is rebellious— it is discontented with its own station and hence rebellious against the law of God. Aurelius hated being ruler of the world, but he bore it patiently since it was the duty God had assigned him. Like Jude, he wanted to be a philosopher and scholar. In citing Aurelius Hardy invokes Stoic doctrine as a text for interpreting Jude's failure and despair: the will of God is equivalent to the law of nature, which in turn is equivalent to reason, and the duty of every human being is to conform to the station in which God has placed him. Aurelius explains the consequences of deviating from the will of God: "For the movement towards injustice and intemperance and to anger and grief and fear is nothing else than the act of one who deviates from nature. And also when the ruling faculty is discontented with anything that happens, then too it deserts its post." Jude's ambition is a sin; since his spirit is rebellious and he is the author of his misfortunes, he should have married and settled down as a stonemason— a point of view that is forcibly contradicted by the dignity and stature Jude achieves through rebellion.

Part Sixth

"At Christminster Again" has two epigraphs. The first is from the book of Esther (14:2): "And she humbled her body greatly, and all the places of her joy she filled with her torn hair." It portrays Sue after the death of her children. In context the passage conveys the idea not of suffering but of power. Hardy quotes from the apocryphal "additions to Esther," the last three chapters of the book, which are traditionally found in the Catholic but not in the Protestant or the Jewish Bible. The Persian king Artaxerxes has issued a decree that the Jews shall be massacred. The Jews, believing this is God's judgment upon them for being unfaithful to the Law, repent in sackcloth and ashes. Among them is Queen Esther, who prays for the Lord to help her change the king's mind: "Remember, O Lord, make thyself known in time of our affliction, and give me boldness, O king of the nations, and Lord of all power. Give me eloquent speech in my mouth before the lion." Her prayers are answered; she puts off her mourning and resumes her royal station; and the king spares the Jews. Esther's humbling is directed toward her people's salvation, whereas Sue's humbling is self-centered and degrading and brings her and Jude nothing but suffering and death.

Hardy takes his final epigraph from Browning's poem "Too Late" in the collection *Dramatis Personae* (1864): "There are two who decline, a woman and I / And enjoy our death in the darkness here."[24] The poem is jeering and embittered, the monologue of a man who has hit bottom out of love for a woman who did not merit his love. The allusion could indicate that Jude dies as an example of romantic desperation, yet Jude declines, not in darkness, but with a mature, clear understanding of his illusions.

5

Conclusions

SUE BRIDEHEAD: THE CASE FOR A FEMINIST READING

In his depiction of Sue, Hardy shows remarkable sensitivity to feminist issues. The novel's tragedy turns on marriage, and it is a double tragedy. This view is augmented by looking into the historical context of women's issues.

In discussing *Jude* in the context of Hardy's fiction as a whole, Patricia Ingham (1989) observes that over the course of his novel writing Hardy's treatment of women increasingly diverges from the traditional misogynist stereotype which had been "scientifically" justified by Herbert Spencer in his popular *The Study of Sociology* (1873).

Owing to the far-reaching influence of Darwin, Spencer's discourse was scientific rather than moral. Darwinism, with *On the Origin of Species* (1859), but more particularly with *The Descent of Man* (1871), gave momentum to biological determinism as it related to the female nature and role. By appealing to so-called objective laws, and adopting a tone of neutral and dispassionate observation, science sought to establish the biological link between physiology, psychology, and sociology, and to effect the ratification of the status quo—that is, to confirm the old stereotypes, and to reaffirm the disabilities of being a woman. This spurious science replaced the Bible as the underpinning of the double standard of sexual morality. Social critics used concepts of evolution to show that sexual difference was the result of adaptation to the conditions necessary for social survival. Woman's position in society was seen as the natural result of processes designed to strengthen her essential function—maternity. Spencer claimed that women had less power than men for abstract thinking because their vital energies went toward nuturing offspring. As a result, women lagged behind men in the evolutionary process, having smaller brains as well as weaker physiques. As the weaker sex, Spencer argued, women had learned to disguise their feelings, to please and persuade, and to delight in submission. Because Victorian women were not only dependent but ready to cultivate and display that dependence, a husband was their only goal. Although in the Victorian period women were often revered as being morally superior—more devout and devoted to caring for others—some writers were of the opinion that woman's reproductive capacity gave her a far more menacing nature. Havelock Ellis, in *Man and Woman* (1894), stated that since menstruation is disgusting, women are ashamed of it, and shame makes them deceitful. This tendency toward dishonesty is, he asserted, reinforced by the duties of maternity, and much of the education of the young, which is entrusted to women, consists of skillful lying.

Childbearing, one of the few acceptable activities for women in Victorian society, dominated women's lives. In 1900 a quarter of all married women in England were pregnant. Most deliveries took place at home, where the experience could be nothing but a struggle with poverty, pain, and death. Stillbirths, miscarriages, attempts at abortion, uncaring doctors, and incompetent midwives caused women to fear pregnancy. The infant death rate in 1900 was 163 per thousand, compared to 9.4 per thousand in 1985. In all, 145,000 infants died in 1900. The medical profession did not explain about or provide contraception or abortion. The condom and vaginal sponge were unreliable and in any case unavailable to most people because birth control was relatively costly. Among the working classes there was a flourishing trade in abortion-inducing pills.

Employment for women outside the home was effectively limited to "women's work"—work that required nimble fingers or no great physical strength, for example, dressmaking, schoolteaching, bar keeping, assisting in a shop, doing office work, or working in domestic service. The telephone, typewriter, and bicycle widened career possibilities for women in the 1890s, but professional opportunities did not exist for women until after the First World War. Therefore the ideal woman was supported by her husband and had no independent legal existence.

The movement to change this state of affairs came to the fore in the last two decades of the nineteenth century, a period during which organized labor was pressing for social and political emancipation. Throughout Europe mass socialist and working-class parties were organizing and demanding fundamental changes. A group of middle-class feminists sponsored debates and campaigned for legislation giving women access to the professions, secondary and higher education, the right to own property, and the right to vote. They crusaded against adult prostitution, the flourishing trade in child prostitution, and the protection of "innocence" that made sexuality furtive and dismal.

By the 1890s the woman question was being widely debated in newspapers, journals, and novels. J. S. Mill had argued in *The Subjection of Women* (1869) that the so-called disabilities of women were maintained in order to make women servants of men who feared the competition of women in the working place, and who could not tolerate living with them as equals. The most popular writer on the woman question, Grant Allen, portrayed marriage as a degrading form of slavery. In his novel, *The Woman Who Did* (1895), the heroine deliberately has a child with her lover whom she refuses to marry, regarding herself as a moral pioneer doomed to martyrdom.

But the whole weight of social orthodoxy brought to bear on maintaining the stereotype was deeply ingrained in the majority of women as well as men, and the women's movement was not able to reach a consensus on most of the feminist issues raised in the 1880s and 1890s. Some writers argued that promiscuity was the path to self-fulfillment; others asserted that such freedom could only come from celibacy. Another point of contention was childbearing. Was it a woman's most sacred calling? Or was it rather an aspect of her degradation? Could fulfillment come from working in the man's world? Or was the man's world a trap for women?

In spite of much debate on the fundamental place of women in society, many women maintained that there was no escape from their established role. In June 1889 more than one hundred well-known women signed their names to the "Appeal against Female Suffrage," which was printed in a leading journal. The appeal stated that women's direct participation in politics "is made impossible either by the disabilities of sex, or by strong formations of custom and habit resting ultimately upon physical difference, against which it is useless to contend."[1] Among those who endorsed the appeal were Beatrice Webb, Mrs. Humphry Ward, Eliza Lynn Linton, Mrs. Matthew Arnold, and Mrs. Leslie Stephen; a supplementary list of two thousand names was added two months later.

A woman might decide to escape the life marked out for her by "the inexorable laws of nature"—that is, the controlling and channelling of her sexuality into marriage—by refusing the sexual dimension of a relationship. According to Penny Boumelha, Sue Bridehead elected this option. Boumelha contends that Sue's situation is confused and confusing because Sue is not sure whether she wants love without sex or sex but not marriage. Yet one must not see her as lacking sexual feeling, Boumelha argues; rather, Sue's actions should be seen as her response to the dilemma of how to have love without "the penalty."[2]

According to Boumelha, whether Sue denies her sexuality or risks pregnancy, she is reduced. Boumelha says that the tragedy is not brought on by her frigidity but by motherhood: "It is motherhood—her own humiliation by the respectable wives who hound her and Jude from their work, Little Father Time's taunting by his schoolmates—that convinces her that 'the world and its ways have a certain worth,' and so begins her collapse into 'enslavement to forms' " (Boumelha, 148). Hardy, Boumelha observes, is alone among writers of stature in drawing attention to motherhood's role in confining women within the nuclear family. Sue's sexuality destroys her, whereas Arabella's, by contrast, helps her survive. Both reject their husbands, take up with other men, sublimate their sexuality into religiosity, and eventually return to their husbands. Yet a crucial point that emerges from the ironic paralleling of Arabella's life with Sue's is that Arabella never plays a maternal role. Whereas Arabella is identified with sexuality and fecundity—she barters her sexuality for security, seducing Jude by flinging a pig's penis at him and pretending to hatch an egg between her breasts—Sue assumes the role of mother—to her own children as well as to Arabella's son. Thus, according to Boumelha, Hardy understands that a woman's freedom depends on remaining free of the maternal role.

Ingham (1989) argues that Hardy gradually developed his sensitivity to the woman question over the course of 25 years of novel writing. She traces the emergence of metaphors in which workingmen suffering from self-devaluation are compared to women, demonstrating that Hardy ever more insistently subverts the social ideal that a woman's self-fulfillment is rooted in self-denial. By the time Hardy wrote *Jude*, the workingman and woman are "two in one," twins who suffer a similar oppression. This affinity in oppression, Ingham says, is highlighted by the emphasis on Jude's and Sue's similarities. Their being cousins on Jude's mother's side, children of a family doomed by a hereditary curse, points up a sameness that is continuously stressed: by the rhyming circumstance of each taking refuge in the other's room, by Sue's actually appearing in Jude's clothes as a kind of double, and most emphatically by Phillotson's view of them as the lovers in Shelley's "The Revolt of Islam"—transcendent beings, martyred in the cause against tyranny.

Jude comes to see himself and Sue as martyred pioneers. They are yanked "back into pre-determined forms of marriage," Boumelha notes, and this is the tragedy (Boumelha, 150). Conventional notions of sanctity and free will are exploded by the novel: neither the home nor the love relationship is a protected zone, and individual acts and intentions cannot reform society.

Boumelha claims that Hardy understood the crucial importance to women of socialized child care, that it was his expressed reason for supporting female suffrage. In his 1906 letter to the Fawcett Society he states that he hopes suffrage would tend "to break up the present pernicious conventions in respect to manners, customs, religion, illegitimacy, the stereotyped household (that it must be the unit of society), the father of a woman's child (that it is anybody's business but the woman's own), except in cases of disease or insanity" (*Letters* 3: 238). The view that unless the institution of marriage is radically changed, women will continue to be enslaved, is also expressed in the novel. Phillotson tells Gillingham, "And yet, I don't see why the woman and the children should not be the unit without the man" (4:4). When faced with the possibility that Little Father Time may not be his child, Jude makes a statement that gives Hardy's position a sharper focus: "The beggarly question of parentage—what is it, after all? What does it matter, when you come to think of it, whether a child is yours by blood or not? All the little ones of our time are collectively the children of us adults of the time, and entitled to our general care" (5:3).

I do not see *Jude* as a novel primarily about marriage, nor do I think of it as "the Sue story" (Boumelha, 138), as Hardy called it in a letter to Florence Henniker. Yet, Boumelha's and Ingham's arguments offer persuasive interpretations that illuminate Sue's life.

Sue's behavior is confused and confusing, which is to say her behavior indicates her self-control. Marrying Jude would invite oppression, yet loving him without marriage would invite the penalties reserved for sinners. Ambivalent, she appears to be coquettish, half inviting his advances, yet sidestepping them. "[E]picene tenderness," "boyish as a Ganymedes" (2:4) are what the love-sick man sees in her external behavior, but he has no clue about what is at issue. Sue wants to be loved, but she cannot bear to lose her freedom.

SHAME

Hardy's alternation of scenes—one on a comic plane, the other tragic; one lofty, the other low; one affirming, the other repudiating—is the novelist's method for grasping the ambiguous real world. Art mirrors life in that both consist of counterpoint, that is, antithesis. However, in *Jude*, where the hero resembles the author, and the parodic scenes are laced with the bitter tones of self-ridicule, psychological explanations for the novel's ambiguities are plausible. There is a private symbolism, a latent content, to which Hardy is responding. Sardonic puns and foreshadowings mock Jude's endeavors, as if the author enjoys predicting his hero's final despair. Jude's and Sue's devastating sense of shame seems out of proportion to their overt circumstances. Hardy was a nonbeliever clinging to Christianity and a lonely man from humble origins who was obsessed with the class status he had gained through marriage. He wrote *Jude* while trapped in these worlds; so possibly the antagonistic points of view toward Jude and Sue express Hardy's schizophrenic attitudes toward faith and class. Possibly Hardy's inability either to damn or to praise Jude and Sue completely express his psychic deadlock; and perhaps Jude's and Sue's sense of shame about their illicit relationship exposes Hardy's deeply held narcissistic and incestuous fantasy.

Undercutting Jude

Milan Kundera speculates that with the rise of the sciences and the loss of a unifying common religion "the world suddenly appeared in its fearsome ambiguity. . . . Thus was born the world of the Modern Era, and with it the novel, the image and model of that world."[3] In the realm of the novel there is no right or wrong. Anna Karenina is neither the victim of a narrow-minded tyrant, nor is Karenin the victim of an immoral woman. There is no either/or. The novelist succeeds in reflecting the world when he succeeds in reflecting the moral ambiguities of life.

Using Kundera's theory about the novel is one way of discussing Hardy's masterful juggling of points of view. *Jude* rouses our indignation against the established order, with its ignorance and injustice; it rouses our love for its defeated hero, fighting his one-sided battle, and at the same time this hero is critically examined and disparaged.

In Part Second, chapter 1 Jude enters the precincts of Christminster on a moonless evening and imagines himself talking to the ghosts of its eminent graduates: philosophers, poets, religious thinkers, scientists, statesmen and historians. The scene vividly dramatizes Jude's eligibility—the appropriateness, the justness of making it possible for workingmen like him to gain admittance. The lines and speeches he knows by heart exemplify the nobility of mind he dreams of emulating. He would be one of the worthy.

Hardy's perspective on Jude shifts radically with the second chapter, where the author's denigration of Jude is imbedded in the language. "Necessary meditations on the actual, including the mean bread-and-cheese question, dissipated the phantasmal for a while, and compelled Jude to smother high thinkings under immediate needs. He had to get up, and seek for work, manual work; the only kind deemed by many of its professors to be work at all" (2:2). "Phantasmal" and "high thinkings" are snide commentaries. Admittance is a pipe dream; he should shake the cobwebs out of his head and do some "real" work. The language digs at university professors, who are dilettantes, a leisured class. The rough, real work is done by those who have to deal with the "mean bread-and-cheese question." Jude might labor in a more dignified way as a stonemason than as a professor. "Passing out into the streets on this errand he found that the colleges had treacherously changed their sympathetic countenances: some were pompous; some had put on the look of family vaults above ground; something barbaric loomed in the masonries of all. The spirits of the great men had disappeared" (2:2).

Momentarily he acknowledges the hopelessness of his enterprise. "Treacherously changed" implies Jude's naïveté, perhaps his nearness to tears. He is shut out: this is not a place for him. "Pompous," "family vaults," and "barbaric" are not expressions of sour grapes but authorial epithets. The dream is fraudulent as well as impossible. Yet there is a sensuousness in Jude's understanding of the craftsmanship of the stonework that puts him deeply in touch with the stonemasons who built and renovate the university: "The numberless architectural pages around him he read, naturally, less as an artist-critic of their forms than as an artizan and comrade of the dead handicraftsmen whose muscles had actually executed those forms. He examined the mouldings, stroked them as one who knew their beginning, said they were difficult or easy in the working, had taken little or much time, were trying to the arm, or convenient to the tool" (2:2). The craftsmen are more noble, more real to Jude than the dry dilettantism of the professors within the walls.

He shakes off his dismay. He has come here to live by work, and crumbling walls mean he will find employment. He makes his way to the workyard of a stonemason.

> He asked for the foreman, and looked among the new traceries, mullions, transoms, shafts, pinnacles, and battlements standing on the bankers half worked, or waiting to be removed. They were marked by precision, mathematical straightness, smoothness, exactitude: there in the old walls were the broken lines of the original idea; jagged curves, disdain of precision, irregularity, disarray.
>
> For a moment there fell on Jude a true illumination; that here in the stone yard was a centre of effort as worthy as that dignified by the name of scholarly study within the noblest of the colleges. But he lost it under stress of his old idea. He would accept any employment which might be offered him on the strength of his late employer's recommendation; but he would accept it as a provisional thing only. This was his form of the modern vice of unrest. (2:2)

Thus Jude is driven, restlessly unstable, toward a hopeless goal, while a profession native to his ability, and of great value and dignity, lies at hand. Christminster has become his "vice," which is to say, 11 years of ardent labor and thought have been a waste of time, a palliative. Moreover, he observes that nothing innovative is being created in the stoneyard because this particular stoneyard is located in Christminster. Christminster is by definition medieval, and the workmanship is limited to mere patching of what has become superseded and irrelevant.

> Having failed to obtain work here as yet he went away, and thought again of his cousin, whose presence somewhere at hand he seemed to feel in wavelets of interest, if not of emotion. How he wished he had that pretty portrait of her! At last he wrote to his aunt to send it. She did so, with a request, however, that he was not to bring

disturbance into the family by going to see the girl or her relations. Jude, a ridiculously affectionate fellow, promised nothing, put the photograph on the mantelpiece, kissed it—he did not know why— and felt more at home. (2:2)

The suddenness of the switch to Sue indicates Jude's instability, his fondness for dreams, not reality. Her photograph cheers him—"the one thing uniting him to the emotions of the living city." Actually, he is not interested in the "living city": obsessed with the "vice of unrest," he is lonely and makes no friends: "Although people moved round him he virtually saw none. . . . But the saints and prophets in the window-tracery, the paintings in the galleries, the statues, the busts, the gurgoyles, the corbel-heads—these seemed to breathe his atmosphere" (2:2).

The Jude in this passage is no hero striding forth to conquer the citadels of learning. He is neither a great dreamer nor a tragic adventurer. Instead he is rather misguided and pathetic. He makes no formal inquiries about admission procedures at the colleges; he picks up information from casual acquaintances. Yet when he finally realizes that matriculation is impossible, that it would cost him 15 years of scrimping, Hardy portrays Jude as a betrayed Christ. Although the advice given him by Tetuphenay perfectly describes Jude's situation, the reader finds it hateful. Hardy depicts Jude not as a man who has been enlightened by Tetuphenay but as a victim who has been rejected by the degrading scheme of things.

Consistently throughout the novel Hardy cannot sustain a case against Jude. His denigrating impulses are contradicted by the love he devotes to his character, and this continual shift in attitude may explain the shifting points of view. It is probably axiomatic that a novel's richness of infectious feeling, the illusion, that is, of life, is made out of contrast.

In Part Fourth, Phillotson consents to let his unhappy wife leave him. He refuses to constrain her in the name of the law, and Hardy's endorsement of his conduct is reinforced both by the epigraph to the novel, and particularly by the epigraph to Part Fourth, which sanctifies

Phillotson's behavior by invoking Milton and the spirit of the gospels. Thus his energetic protest against dismissal from his teaching post is noble and righteous. But Hardy is already undermining him. When he calls a public meeting to present his high-minded views, he is weak and ill. His champions are disreputable, and Hardy describes them with mischievous irony: "The body included two cheap-jacks, a shooting-gallery proprietor and the ladies who loaded the guns, a pair of boxing-masters, a steam-roundabout manager, two travelling broom-makers, who called themselves widows, a gingerbread-stall keeper, a swing-boat owner, and a 'test-your strength' man" (4:6). After the idiotic and violent farce that develops, Phillotson falls into serious illness and despair. Not only are his prospects ruined; ultimately his admirable rectitude contributes to ruining Jude and Sue.

The depiction of Little Father Time's face after the murders and suicide blames Jude and Sue for his tragedy.

> The boy's face expressed the whole tale of their situation. On that little shape had converged all the inauspiciousness and shadow which had darkened the first union of Jude, and all the accidents, mistakes, fears, errors of the last. He was their nodal point, their focus, their expression in a single term. For the rashness of those parents he had groaned, for their ill-assortment he had quaked, and for the misfortunes of these he had died. (6:2)

Hardy says that Jude and Arabella never should have had this child, and Jude and Sue never should have had their illegitimate children. Yet Hardy's guilty verdict is counterbalanced by his sympathy for Jude, his hatred of orthodoxy, and his contempt for Sue's Christian repentence, which Hardy considers much more of a betrayal than the lovers' defiance of convention.

Novelists are necessarily makers of ambiguity. This means that interpretation to a large extent is subjective. Are Jude and Sue misguided and pathetic, or are they brave and touching? Hardy's juggling of point of view is, to quote Kundera, the novelist's way "of unmasking the world as an ambiguity" (Kundera, 135). The mirage of life is created out of the fabric of counterpoint. Nevertheless, the extent of Hardy's undercutting is extreme, almost pathological.

Conclusions

Jude is the most rigorously and symmetrically constructed of Hardy's novels, its remarkable symmetries imposing a fatalistic design upon the action. It has the form of a geometric pattern of reversals and failures, with the four main characters ending where they began. It appears like an hourglass turning upside down six separate times, with hope emptying into despair until there is no more resilience. The subtext expresses the idea that life is a closed system where one's end is in one's beginning, and the struggle for integrity is futile.

In Part First, chapter 6 Jude walks beside a hedge, deep in concentration, reciting a list of authors he intends to read at Christminster. The recitation is punctuated by a choric refrain, "hoity-toity," coming from over the hedge, and ends when Jude receives a slap on the ear with a pig's pizzle. This scene is darkly echoed by the choric "hurrahs" punctuating Jude's lament at the end of the novel, his recitation from Job which ends in death.

Sue begins in service to religion working in an ecclesiastical shop and will end in service to religion. The prefiguration lies in her pagan deities, Apollo and Venus, which she misrepresents as Saints Peter and Mary Magdalene—predicting the later collapse of her intellect and the repudiation of her sexuality. These foreshadowings are everywhere. Sue is a white heap after she jumps from the connubial bedroom window into freedom, nonconformity, and wifely misconduct. She is a black heap at the foot of the cross in St. Silas' Church, where she repents her willfulness.

Jude's identification with the birds in Troutham's cornfield is an expression of his spiritual being, an inner self given to mental and physical flights, combining Joseph the dreamer with the tragic adventurer Don Quixote. Birds and eggs appear symbolically throughout the novel in contexts of betrayal and failure. Arabella seduces Jude by playing a game with the cochin's egg. Phillotson is championed by carnival people, representatives of unconventional life, who are described as perching at Shaston, their winter resting place, like "strange wild birds" (4:1). The schoolmaster's generosity is a wild flight that costs him his career, respectability, and his principles. Sue is the "little bird . . . caught at last" after she sleeps with Jude. Arabella nests Vilbert's love potion made of dove's hearts in her bosom at a fair; this action refers back to her seduction with the cochin's egg and looks ahead to the entrapment of Jude in a second marriage. Sue rescues her pet doves from the poulterer, but they cannot escape entrapment by Vilbert, who will keep them in his dovecot and slaughter them. When the murdered children are discovered, Jude is timing the boiling of eggs, having earlier, at breakfast, called Sue "my bird." The watch he holds recalls Vilbert, the symbolic timepiece of the old order.

Consistently, pigs are identified with the degradation of Jude's dream and the squalid, real life he is fated to lead. His musings, when he feels orphaned in a world that does not want him, when he wishes he could "prevent himself from growing up" (1:2), occur beside a pigsty. Pig genitals call his attention to Arabella, the daughter of a pig slaughterer, "a complete and substantial female animal" (1:6). The chase of the long-legged pig leads Jude and Arabella to a spot where a caterpillar crawls on a tree, beneath which Arabella lies panting for love. "O, I can see such a pretty thing up this tree," she says, trying to induce him to lie down beside her (1:8). This scene is a picture of the Fall, showing us where the old Adam, the flesh, Jude's runaway pig, is leading him. The graphic coarseness of the pig killing scene symbolizes Jude's degradation with Arabella. She soils his books with hot grease, flinging them to the floor bespattered with lard. Whither has fled the visionary gleam? It is wallowing in gore. In the book burning scene, when in the flames of his illicit passion for Sue he destroys Jeremy Taylor, Cardinal Newman, and his life's venture of becoming an apostle, Jude is standing near a pigsty. When he is entrapped a second time by Arabella, his undoing is set in the bedroom above her father's little pork shop. The symbolism has acquired a meaning: Jude has been born for slaughter.

Phillotson's piano also symbolizes Jude's defeated dream. It witnesses his disappointment when the schoolmaster departs for Christminster. It serves as Jude's envoy, carrying his letter to Phillotson in its packingcase, asking for the magical grammars that would enable him to transpose "all words of his own speech into those of the foreign one" (1:4). The piano shows up at the schoolhouse in Shaston where Jude and Sue play the hymn "The Foot of the Cross." It performs the magic of bringing them together, but the piano also plays out their future tragedy. One supposes that the piano finally ends up with Phillotson in the schoolroom at Marygreen where it began.

Other ironies are revealed in Hardy's play on words and names. Jude wanted to be a don, and he marries Arabella, whose father is named Donn. Little Father Time's suicide note, "Done because we are too menny," contains what sounds like a sarcastic pun—Don Tetuphenay—pointing out the folly of bucking convention. Hardy probably named Jude after St. Jude Thaddeus, the patron saint of hopeless, impossible, and difficult cases.

Fatalism is the emotional expression of the novel's constricting design. It is also an expression of something that the characters themselves represent to Hardy: an image of deadlock—something anxiety-producing and taboo in nature that is depicted by the tragedy and most symptomatically revealed by Jude's and Sue's potent sense of shame. Sue lives with one eye looking back over her shoulder, fearful of retributive consequences. Her life is a series of penances. Jude's life is a perpetual struggle with feelings of shame and worthlessness. After his dismissal by Farmer Troutham, he wishes he had never been born. A few months after marrying Arabella, he feels like one of the "despairing worthless" and attempts to drown himself (1:11). On first spying Sue, he thinks of himself as "cross-grained, unfortunate, almost accursed stock" (2:2). After the dismissive letter from Tetuphenay, he goes on a binge, "convinced that he was at bottom a vicious character, of whom it was hopeless to expect anything" (2:7). On returning to Marygreen at the end of Part Second, he is left in "the hell of conscious failure." Feelings of worthlessness again overpower Jude after Sue's marriage to Phillotson, when for "a ghastly half hour of depression" he feels suicidal (3:8). On returning to Christminster in Part Sixth, his sense of failure and pariahdom is extreme. These feelings are pervasive and potent, suggesting that they have a basis in the author's life.

An Agnostic's and Parvenu's Apology The novel's shifting point of view expresses a deeply schizophrenic attitude toward middle-class values, revealing a psychological pattern of ambivalence about class and crossing class barriers, a zigzag pattern that records Hardy's inner struggle to express both admiration and hostility for the middle class. Similarly, the novel's tensions mirror Hardy's and the Victorian age's ambivalence toward religion: a desire to adhere to the traditional creed and an acknowledgment that the old faith has been compromised by Darwinian theory. It may be that the ironic richness and deep pathos of the novel derive from Hardy's ability to combine contradictory worlds—London and Dorchester, faith and science—and that if there is psychological meaning in his technique of composition, it lies in the counterpointing that expresses the paralyzing ambivalence that Hardy seemed to cultivate in order to write.

Jude the Obscure records the profound personal and social dilemmas of a writer who attempts to exonerate himself from the subversive implications of his text. Its inherent contradictions image Hardy's own ambivalence about the forces challenging his society at the turn of the century: the new working-class and feminist movements that demanded fundamental social changes, and the influence of Darwinian thought, which threatened to overthrow Christianity. Hardy was at heart a country clergyman who could not sustain a case for or against Jude's middle-class ambitions; for or against Sue's fear of marriage; or for or against the Church. Jude and Sue act out the anxiety-ridden dilemmas of late Victorians who face an insentient universe they fear and cling to a Christian world order that is collapsing.

Fear of Darwin's new theory prompted Samuel Wilberforce, the Lord Bishop of Oxford, to denigrate Darwin's argument in two articles, which he published after the famous debate with Thomas Henry Huxley. The Lord Bishop expressed admiration for Darwin as a scientist, that is, as an observer and experimenter. He said that he accepted the principle of natural selection—that a struggle for life actually exists, and that the strong, or better adapted, supplant the weak—though he deliberately misinterpreted the idea that each slight variation of usefulness is preserved, calling it God's mechanism for mercifully preventing deterioration. But Darwin's argument is not amenable to religious interpretation. The idea that natural selection produces new species, that all of life, including human beings, is descended from one primordial form, diminishes the glory of God. That Darwin's theory contradicts God's relation to man was the crux of Wilberforce's bitter opposition. He well understood how disturbing Darwin's speculations would be to people raised in the comforts of faith. How were they to confront a universe governed by mechanistically determined laws? The paltriness of man's place in its scheme and the amoral nature of events are profoundly dangerous to faith. If Christianity is false, prayer is useless; the soul is not immortal; there are no future rewards and punishments, and the floodgates are open to every kind of radicalism. Religion, after all, is a form of social control; without the traditional sanctions of religion the foundations of public life could be shaken. Life without Christianity would be a meaningless, valueless chaos.

Inevitably, popular novelists like Eliza Lynn Linton and Mrs. Humphry Ward wrote best-sellers exploiting the shock value of these anxieties. Linton wrote, "[I]f the law of the struggle for existence and the survival of the fittest applies absolutely to human society as well as to plants and fishes, let us then be frank, and candidly admit that Christianity . . . is a craze. . . . Jesus of Nazareth preached and prac-tised not only in vain, but against unchangeable Law" (quoted in Harrison, 127). By the last decades of the century, the intellectual force of Darwinism had made it increasingly difficult for educated Christians to believe what the church had taught for so long. The Bible may not be literally true. The moral world order may be a fable. The human race may not be descended from Adam and Eve. One of the moral pillars of Victorian society, Leslie Stephen, in *An Agnostic's Apology* (1893), defended the reasons for his skepticism. But arguments did not diminish public anxiety. Received opinion yielded—the majority of people made some kind of mental accommodation—but hardly gave ground. Even a majority of zoologists, biologists, and paleontologists did not accept natural selection as the prime cause of evolutionary change until the 1930s.

Darwin himself became sick with anxiety as he secretly began to espouse in a series of pocket notebooks doctrines that threatened the whole fabric of inherited belief. In many respects Darwin seems a prototype for Hardy. Darwin appeared destined to become a country clergyman when he entered Cambridge in 1828, and he never formally gave up his intention of seeking ordination. After making his way around the world on a ten-gun brig, "[h]e had begun to articulate a vision of the world in which all living things were linked together through natural generation over vast eons of time; and not only their physical structures, but their habits, instincts, reasoning power, emotions, morality, and even belief in God."[4] "How far grander than idea from cramped imagination that God created" (quoted in Moore, 457), Darwin scrawled in his notebook in 1838. How beneath the dignity of God was biblical creation compared to his own "magnificent view" (quoted in Moore, 456). But such entries gave him palpitations, indigestion, and headaches. He condemned himself as a flagrant social offender, and he feared the censure and persecution of fellow naturalists. He was also anxious about his wife, Emma, a devout evangelical unitarian, who knew that he had been intended for the Church. Darwin moved to a quiet country parish eight miles from a train station, where he and his family lived more or less in seclusion for forty years. After 1859, when his books and reputation were constantly before the public eye, he had prolonged bouts of ill-health and was extensively involved in parish life: he served on the school committee, sponsored a reading room and public lectures, acted as treasurer for the Sunday School, and became a magistrate. In short, he upheld the existing order of society, demonstrating deep respect for authority of all kind, while at the same time challenging the status quo.

In many respects Hardy was like Darwin: intensely ambivalent, secretive, anxious about respectability—one who upheld the existing order yet subverted the status quo. Although he stopped believing in Christianity while in his middle twenties, Hardy continued to love the language of the Bible and the beauty of church services: he was a sort of muddled theist to the end. He, too, had had a dream of becoming a country clergyman. Prospective candidates were expected to go to Oxbridge for three years to become educated as gentlemen and spend a fourth year attending voluntary lectures on theology and preparing themselves for ordination. The average Anglican clergyman had a wife and a carriage, and the young Hardy's vision of the future probably included a handsome rectory complete with well-laid lawns, a gardener, a housekeeper, and a groom. In a different society it should have been possible for an exceptional young man, who was self-taught, ascetic, and dedicated; but it was a pipedream for the 75 percent of the population who, like him, belonged to the working class. Even though young Hardy, like his hero Jude, belonged to the working-class aristocracy—artisans and tradesmen enjoying good wages and steady employment—there was no way he could have acquired an Oxbridge degree. That bitter knowledge, which was internalized as hatred of the Church for buttressing the restrictive laws of a class society, is one of the primary motives of *Jude*, along with a stubborn, nagging longing for lost faith.

Hardy wrote *Jude* when he was a respectable member of the middle class scrupulously concealing his connection to an extended family of bricklayers. At that time, he had not associated with his relatives for 20 years. Unlike Jude, Hardy married a woman from the upper middle class and rose to eminence, surmounting class barriers and establishing himself in society. But this success story had an ironic twist. In realizing his dream, Hardy cut himself off from his roots. He found himself belonging nowhere, tensely guarded in society and aloof and secretive at home. His marriage to Emma became an irritant to both of them, a sexless companionship that intensified his sense of loneliness and increased his craving for idealized love. Like Jude, he half believed himself doomed by some hereditary curse. He came from a family with a history of misalliances. Bitter, lonely men attracted him, men with doomed careers, like his uncle John Antell (a shoemaker and a self-taught amateur classical scholar who died frustrated and alcoholic) and his mentor Horace Moule (a brilliant but failed Cambridge man who remained single and finally cut his throat). These men had great promise but came to nothing. Once married, Hardy seems to have conspired with a fate he could not alter. He cultivated loneliness: having previously felt at home with his numerous relatives, he abruptly broke all ties with them. The Fawley curse fictionalizes this aspect of his life. Having achieved a place in society, he became paralyzed by strategies adopted to conceal his origins. Although he learned to play billiards, dressed smartly, studied books on social etiquette and genealogy, and referred to his home in Dorchester as a getaway cottage, he could not hide his working-class nuances of speech and behavior. He walked cautiously through society, masked in fictions and always half-expecting to be snubbed. Social insecurity made him suffer terribly from criticism, and he never forgave his closest literary adviser and friend, Edmund Gosse, for telling him to his face that "*Jude* was the most indecent novel ever written" (Millgate 1982, 373). To be able to write, he may have needed to nourish his creativity by feeding on the pervasive guilt and loneliness within himself. It is no surprise that he brings to Jude's ambition his own contradictory emotions, the bitter bemusement of a chronicler who has bitten deeply of the poison apple of success.

Hardy's marriage in 1874 to an archdeacon's niece provided him with an entrée into the upper echelons of London society. But in time, as he became a distinguished novelist, he realized that Emma was a social buffoon, lacking tact, taste, and wit. She, too, in time realized that she was not acceptable in society.

In 1882 Hardy established his wife in Dorchester, where in 1885 he built Max Gate, needing contact with the scenes of his rural youth to nourish his imagination. He was an hour's walk from his mother's house and visited her every Sunday, yet Emma was never permitted there. Ironically, having married to enlarge his horizons—having given up an extended family of aunts and uncles and cousins in order to be acceptable in society—he found himself with a wife whom his mother rejected, and since they had no children, his personal circle became very small indeed. In Dorchester, he and Emma had no common social life. They went to church together, but it was a mockery of togetherness since he had lost his faith and she was increasingly dogmatic.

After his marriage, Hardy ceases to mention his relatives in any of his notes and writings. He would bicycle stiffly down the high street of Puddletown, where his mother's numerous sisters and their families lived, without greeting anyone. Emma chafed at being tucked away in a small town, imprisoned in a marriage with a secretive man. Jemima Hardy, her mother-in-law, an exceedingly possessive mother, disliked her, accusing her of being a prig without a pedigree; the two women did not meet until three years after the marriage. A total break between the two households occurred in 1892, after which even Hardy's sisters and brother did not visit Max Gate.

Yet, for a time, Emma shared Hardy's work. She regarded herself as a novelist and was, in fact, an indispensable helpmate. She read and commented on his early drafts. Together they compiled voluminous notebooks filled with vivid phrases, aphorisms, news items, curious facts— all the entries were set off and numbered, ready to be used in his novels. She wrote out his drafts in longhand. But she did not feel appreciated for helping him achieve his literary success, and for giving him an entrée into London society. Through her, the son of a stonemason and a cook, the man her father had written off as "a base churl,"[5] entered a social world that occasionally included royalty, yet she eventually felt excluded from it. All their differences came to a head with the publication of *Jude*, after which she quit helping him with his work entirely.

No wonder Hardy was confused about class allegiance. His life was "a many layered and schizophrenic obsession" (Widdowson, 147) with social status, which made for sardonic and contradictory attitudes toward Jude. His own ambition to rise had cut him off from his roots and left him deeply alienated, isolated with his fantasies like "a gherkin in its vinegar" (Flaubert). But his ambivalence is like a rapidly changing tide. The dykes break, he swells with indignant love for Jude, and the depiction is swamped by hostility toward the class system. This counterpoint between comic derision and tragic indignation, farce and melancholy, constitutes the fundamental texture of the novel.

A Paradise of Despair The bitterness between Hardy and Emma dates from 1891 when Hardy achieved the peak of social standing through *Tess*'s popularity. At this time, as a man of distinction, he enjoyed aristocratic gatherings where he was recognized, welcomed, and solaced for his loveless marriage. He began to enjoy the company of young, rich, attractive women, and Emma began keeping a secret diary to which she confided her various complaints against her husband.

In *The Pursuit of the Well-Beloved*, serialized in 1892, Hardy

JUDE AT THE MILE-STONE

fictionalizes the tragicomedy of his life with what must have seemed to Emma bewildering brutality. In the novel, the wife believes she has married beneath her, and the husband believes that since he has achieved fame as an artist, she should be content to bask in his glory. In the final episode, after a series of fruitless romances, the hero laughs hysterically at his aging body yoked to an ugly wife: "Oh—no, no! I—I—it is too, too droll—this ending to my would-be romantic history." The novel closes with the exclamation, "Ho-ho-ho!"—a bitter chuckle set off outside quotation marks, and hence authorial (Millgate 1982, 331). Not only did Hardy supplant Emma with a series of attractive protégées, but he also proclaims, through the fictional husband, that his wife disgusts him.

"Love lives on propinquity, but dies of contact," Hardy wrote in the summer of 1889 (*Life*, 230). Like an adolescent in and out of love, his attractions to titled, literary ladies all began feverishly and were soon exhausted; passionate letter writing always ended in friendship. His well-beloved of 1893, Florence Henniker, was a slim, graceful woman in her late thirties, the married sister of Lord Houghton, the Lord-Lieutenant of Ireland. The love triangles of *Jude the Obscure* took form during Hardy's highly charged emotional involvement with her—Phillotson serving as his superego who rises above convention to permit the extramarital affair then succumbs to convention in order to kill it off. From Emma's point of view, Hardy's political ideas about the constricting effects of marriage were the public ravings of a man who would like to be free but is too traditional, so he fantasizes about magical, unconsummated affairs.

Jude the Obscure, a shadow resemblance of Hardy's inner life, reveals his loss of faith, his loneliness in the midst of social success, his unhappy married life, and his craving for magical love. Hardy's extreme emotional dependence on his mother, his surrender to her "all-encompassing influence and direction" (Millgate 1982, 23), leads his biographer to compare Hardy's mother, Jemima, with the mother in D. H. Lawrence's autobiographical *Sons and Lovers*. Young Hardy, like Paul Morel, suffered from prolonged immaturity and was in his own estimate "a child till he was sixteen, a youth till he was five-and-twenty, and a young man till he was nearly fifty" (*Life*, 37). He was extremely delicate. When he was born, the doctor thought he was dead and set him aside. Gittings describes him as "a solemn small boy, odd-looking and with a big head, carrying a full satchel of books" (Gittings 1975, 21). His mother was the driving force behind his insatiable pursuit of knowledge—his instinctive impulse for the life of the mind and the world of books. The tenacity of the maternal hold seems evident in the circumstance of Hardy's relationship to three of his cousins—the three daughters of his mother's eldest sister, Maria Sparks. In his early twenties he proposed to Martha Sparks, who was six years older than he. Earlier he had made adolescent advances to her eldest sister, Rebecca. In his late twenties he became engaged to Tryphena, a younger version of Rebecca and Martha, and a model for Sue. She was completing the three years of pupil teaching that would qualify her for training college when they were courting in the late 1860s. Apparently Hardy was falling in love with his mother over and over again. His biographers say that he was sexually curious about almost every woman he met, attracted to the idea of love yet lacking the capacity or desire to satisfy or realize it.

If, as the British novelist John Fowles says, the artistic process itself is a "doomed and illicit hunt" for the early experience of oneness with the mother (Fowles, 35), in *Jude the Obscure* Hardy's Oedipal fantasy is extraordinarily out in the open. Fowles says that Hardy "had not yet fully seen his 'sickness' " until he wrote *The Well-Beloved*, which appeared in serial publication just before he began *Jude* (Fowles, 30). By "sickness," he means Hardy's obsessive longing for a young female whose love symbolizes "a unified magical world" of childhood (Fowles, 31). Her attraction is "erotic elusiveness, unattainability" because she is an incarnation of the unattainable mother (Fowles, 34). There can be no happy ending, no symbolic marriage between "hero-author and heroine-mother" (Fowles, 35). Thus, in *Jude*, the pressure of longing is not for consummation but for postponement, Hardy finding his deepest pleasure in the "endlessly repeated luring-denying nature of his [heroine]," whom Fowles calls a "cock-tease" (Fowles, 36). He says further that "malign coincidence and class difference" are obstacles invented by Hardy to prolong the pleasure of "the hunt," of being possessed by his Oedipal fantasy (Fowles, 35).

It is no wonder, then, that *Jude* contains so much pessimism and fatalism, farcical passages that seethe with self-mockery, derisive epigraphs, and a muted undercurrent of shame, of something taboo-ridden about Jude's desires. In this last of Hardy's novels, we can see the author hiding behind Jude. Sue is his hopeless, guilt-ridden obsession, his transmogrified memory of infancy when his identity was merged with that of his mother. Arabella is his flirtation with adult sexuality and his inevitable disgust for it. And Phillotson is the frustrater of the dream, the Oedipal father. The novel gives us some clues to the private man (who quit novel writing for the greater privacy of poetry after *Jude*) and offers a psychic framework for understanding why the surrogate heroes in his earlier masterpieces are stunted. Possibly this last novel has the profound importance, as some argue, of exposing a social neurosis, Jude's love for Sue representing a cultural fantasy. Read in this way, the novel is an allegory of everyman's repression of the erotic impulse and of the creative/destructive power of this particular stranglehold.

Hardy's multiple perspectives work to defend Jude and Sue from censure—Hardy is concerned with winning our sympathy for this love which is narcissistic and debilitating. We see, we feel, we know everything, and yet nothing: for the multiple perspectives neutralize our ability to moralize, and we are caught in something equivalent to Jude's compulsion. This is the marvel of the work, that a paradise of despair is created out of a neurotic compulsion, a blindness to reality, a blindness that ennobles and elevates as well as destroys.

There is good evidence for seeing Sue as coequal to Jude, a sympathetic victim crushed by forces more insidious than those Jude encounters. It can be argued that she is not coquettish or frigid, but that her refusal of the sexual dimension is a necessary stand against being reduced as a human being, and that her active sexuality is a decisive element in her collapse. Yet Sue is made the instrument of Jude's downfall rather than the subject of her own. Intellectualize as we will, we are disgusted by her grovelling collapse. D. H. Lawrence, to whom Christianity was the greatest enemy of the intuitive life, saw its effects personified in Sue. Deracinated, frightened of her sexuality, she embodies the frenzy that results from repressed impulses. Jude's love for her is a symptom of the same psychic disorder, which is responsible, in Lawrence's thinking, for industrialization and the disintegration of society. Lawrence read literature as symbolic spiritual autobiography in which the author struggles against his culture.

Lawrence felt extremely close to Hardy, whom he read as his literary precursor. According to him, Hardy's masterpieces before *Jude* are psychic dramas symbolizing the destructive influence of fastidious and idealistic men—Hardy surrogates—on unusually vital women. It seems to me that the psychic twist in *The Return of the Native*, for instance, lies in the improbable accidents of the plot that reveal Clym's hidden character. His sudden loss of sight and disregard for Eustacia correspond to an emotional constrictedness suggesting impotence. He works as a faggot cutter from four in the morning until nine at night, napping a few hours in the afternoon. His mind is asleep; he is peaceful in the womb of nature—and this is why he has returned from Paris to live on Egdon Heath, near his mother. Passionate Eustacia and his mother are antagonists and emblems of his divided soul.

In *The Mayor of Casterbridge*, a powerful and masculine figure undergoes a grotesque atonement for his virility. The psychic twist is the same—that is, the sadistic destruction of a vital person. Although Lawrence did not know the details of Hardy's personal life, he accurately inferred Hardy's personality from his fictional heroes. The details, as we know them now, fit Lawrence's profile, that is, of a man caught in the stranglehold of narcissistic and incestuous fantasies—his close bond to his mother, his love for three successive cousins on his mother's side—all affecting his behavior—his sexual flirtations and lack of sexual involvement, and the family legend that he was sexually impotent.

Finally *Tess*, which precedes *Jude*, is a variation on the theme of a vital person destroyed by a sexually inhibited one. There is a straight line from Clym, to Angel, to Sue, illustrating the perversions created by Christianity. Lawrence realized this while writing his book on Hardy's novels in 1914, and it was a discovery of profound importance to him as a creative artist, for it enabled him to make the bridge from *Sons and Lovers* (1913) to *The Rainbow* (1915)—to seeing that the family tragedy described in his autobiographical novel was a collective problem and part of a larger social pathology. To Lawrence, the whole human effort toward life in the spirit, that is, the tragedy of Christianity, is imaged in the spiritualized, debilitating love of Jude and Sue. This is part of a seductive metaphysic that has greatly influenced Hardy criticism.

I think that a central idea in Lawrence's *Study of Thomas Hardy* is that the clog in Hardy's would-be lovers—surrogates such as Clym and Angel—is the neurosis exposed in Jude's love for Sue. *Jude the Obscure* can be read as a psychic drama about deadlock. The style of neutralizing perspectives, the novel's numerous paradoxes, all create a deadlocked state. The old town of Marygreen is neither picturesque nor modern; progress has merely obliterated its individuality. Social advances that encourage independent thought and action and freedom from superstition are cancelled out by restlessness, chaos, and despair. This very real deadlock was a factor in Hardy's private life. He could not return to a nostalgic past, nor had he a way out of his loneliness, either in being single like Moule or in being married. Psychologically, as well as socially, the novel is structured on the idea of paralysis— the shame, that is, of a love that is both life and poison.

This idea, that Hardy exposes in *Jude* the sterility of his own crippling fantasy while at the same time idealizing it, is similar to the novelist John Fowles's (1977) and Michael Steig's Freudian analyses of the novel. Steig says that Hardy bases *Jude* on Shelley's "The Revolt of Islam," the novel roughly following the poem.[6] In "The Revolt of Islam" the male protagonist journeys to a visionary city where he rescues a beautiful woman from a degrading sexual enslavement. Cythna dominates her lover intellectually. They are far in advance of their time, living by their own moral code. They leave the city together and unite sexually, an act so intense it lasts two days. When at the end of the poem they return to the visionary city, they are burned as martyrs.

Steig conjectures that Hardy read Shelley's poem as an incest fantasy. Laon and Cythna were originally brother and sister. "[T]hat Cythna makes love enthusiastically even when famished for food is the kind of event that can take place only in a work that does not claim to portray the real world" (Steig, 194). She is the type of "seraph of heaven" that Shelley was repeatedly falling in love with, the same type that Hardy found attractive—epicene, ethereal, equivocally sexual, with the ability to keep a man's passion hot. This female quality, Steig says, is what Hardy saw attracting Laon to Cythna, and it is what attracted him, and Jude, to types like Sue. The operative fantasy in both poem and novel is the woman's ability to rouse her lover's desire for her "simultaneously because of her sexuality and because of her purity—to provide the attraction of incest" along with "the phantasied permanent chasteness": in other words, an Oedipal fantasy (Steig, 194).[7] Shelley does not have to face the psychological consequences of his fantasy; in his poem it becomes a spiritualized sexual passion that achieves total union in a visionary realm. But Hardy is compelled in the novel to dramatize the consequences of his fantasy in actual human life, and more specifically, in terms of his own actual life. Hence the self-derisive mockery, parody, and pessimism.

■ ■ ■

Milan Kundera says that the compulsion to get to the heart of the mystery of a text reflects an inability to tolerate ambiguity, to accept, that is, "the essential relativity of things human" (Kundera, 7). In the universe of the novel, however, moral certainties are impossible; the novel is by definition the ironic art, and "irony doesn't give a damn about messages" (Kundera, 139). These remarks constitute a plea not to use literature to moralize, and not to obscure the contradictions in a text in the service of theory.

Novelists direct their energies into their work driven on by a need to transform their anxieties into phrases, into the concentrated activity of writing. Shouts of victory—immunity from disaster, that is—last only so long as they can keep it up. In one important respect Hardy in *Jude the Obscure* is closer to the postmodern spirit of Gabriel Garcia-Marquez and Salman Rushdie than to the Victorian age. I am referring to his laughter—his black laughter—but one senses that had he been born 20 years later, he might have been able to turn Schopenhauer on his head. In all its details life is a comedy, Schopenhauer says, a comedy that robs life of whatever dignity it might have had, degrading an otherwise meaningless tragedy.[8] Had Hardy been born a quarter of a century later, the comedy of mishaps, chance meetings, the quirky twists of life, might have ignited exuberance, flights of hilarious and grotesque whimsy, a burlesque of tragic emotions. Still, I sense in *Jude* a pressure to break out that is depressed and grounded yet responsible for a marvelous visionary energy constrained by the author's shame at still needing his mother, and the mother church.

Hardy shares George Eliot's view of "wise passiveness" as the safest course of action in an age in which there are no universal affirmations and no binding beliefs. In such an age, the protagonist's desire for authentic existence is defeated by forces of established law, and stoic acceptance passes for virtue. Yet Hardy's tragic vision is heroic; it allies itself with the sufferer, since the author identifies with his protagonist's hopeless striving. Hardy is working in two modes at once, the comic and the tragic. He is suspicious of the noble hero, the grand gesture, the inflated ego; he takes a lively satisfaction in forecasting Jude's doom. The tragic visionary is a fool for imagining he can create his own order. Hardy cannot tolerate transgressors, but he celebrates them. Jude's soul becomes toughened and strengthened by his battle against destiny. In defeat, he is superior to the forces of religion and morality. We identify with his indignation and feel a defiant sympathy with him when he perseveres.

Yeats wrote, "I saw what should have been plain from the first line I had written, that tragedy must always be a drowning and breaking of the dykes that separate man from man, and that it is upon these dykes comedy keeps house."[9] As Yeats's metaphor implies, the comic mode is insular and safe, resting on the dikes, whereas the tragic mode risks annihilation, demanding emotional sensitivity and engagement. In his comic vein, Hardy walls himself off from suffering. At times the novel appears more sardonic than compassionate, but we are never freed from the preoccupation with human anguish and the human condition—never freed from the bittersweet torture of participating in Jude's doomed struggle.[10]

Notes and References

1. HISTORICAL CONTEXT

1. Robert Gittings, *Young Thomas Hardy*, vol. 1 (Boston: Little, Brown & Co., 1975), 48; hereafter cited in the text.

2. Michael Millgate, *Thomas Hardy: A Biography* (New York: Random House, 1982), 108; hereafter cited in the text.

3. As quoted in Leonard Huxley's *Life and Letters of Thomas Henry Huxley*, vol. 1 (London: Macmillan, 1900), 185.

4. For instance, Mill writes, "No one can be a great thinker who does not recognise, that as a thinker it is his first duty to follow his intellect to whatever conclusions it may lead. Truth gains more even by the errors of one who, with due study and preparation, thinks for himself, than by the true opinions of those who only hold them because they do not suffer themselves to think" (*On Liberty: Annotated Text, Sources and Background Criticism*, ed. David Spitz [New York: Norton, 1975], 33; hereafter cited in the text).

For one of the most thorough cultural histories of the period, see Noel Annan, *Leslie Stephen: A Godless Victorian*.

5. *Jude the Obscure*, ed. Norman Page (New York and London: Norton, 1978), part 6, chapter 2; subsequent citations appear in the text; the first number cited parenthetically refers to the part number, and the number after the colon refers to the chapter number.

6. David Cecil, *Hardy the Novelist: An Essay in Criticism* (London: Constable & Co., 1943), 156; hereafter cited in the text.

7. See especially Penny Boumelha's opening chapter, "Sexual Ideology and the 'Nature' of Woman 1880–1900" in her book on Hardy, *Thomas Hardy and Women: Sexual Ideology and Narrative Form* (Sussex: Harvester Press, 1982).

3. CRITICAL RECEPTION

1. *The Life and Work of Thomas Hardy,* ed. Michael Millgate (London: Macmillan, 1984), 216; hereafter cited in the text as *Life.*

2. *Thomas Hardy's Personal Writings: Prefaces, Literary Opinions, Reminiscences,* ed. Harold Orel (Lawrence: University of Kansas Press, 1966), 32; hereafter cited in the text as *Personal Writings.*

3. In order to make his novel suitable for family consumption, Hardy was obliged to make some of the following changes for magazine publication. Arabella inveigles rather than seduces Jude into marriage by pretending to have another lover. Sue and Jude do not live together in Aldbrickham but live in houses on either side of a narrow street, and when Jude comes in to breakfast, they shake hands rather than kiss. They adopt children rather than have illegitimate ones, and so on.

4. R. G. Cox, ed. *Thomas Hardy: The Critical Heritage* (New York: Barnes & Noble, 1970), 257; hereafter cited in the text.

5. In Lawrence's theory, Hardy failed to see that Christianity was his enemy and to blame for his destructive obsession with idealized love. *Study of Thomas Hardy* appears in *Phoenix: The Posthumous Papers of D. H. Lawrence,* ed. Edward D. McDonald (New York: Viking Press, 1972); hereafter cited in the text as *Phoenix.*

6. E. M. Forster, *Aspects of the Novel* (New York: Harcourt Brace & World, 1954), 141; hereafter cited in the text.

7. Virginia Woolf, *The Common Reader: Second Series* (London: Hogarth Press, 1932), 255; hereafter cited in the text.

8. William R. Rutland, *Thomas Hardy: A Study of His Writings and Their Background* (New York: Russell & Russell, 1962), 256; hereafter cited in the text.

9. Walter Allen uses Lawrence's analysis to argue that Hardy's pessimistic novels are "arraignment[s] of the nature of the universe as he saw it." He says, "[b]elieving that where man was concerned the very nature of things was malign, he believed also that it was the more malign the more sensitive, the more intelligent, the more finely organized the human being. The only characters in Hardy who need fear no fall are those already down, those who live close to earth without aspirations to rise" (*The English Novel: A Short Critical History* [New York: E.P. Dutton, 1957], 289).

10. Phyllis Bartlett, " 'Seraph of Heaven': A Shelleyan Dream in Hardy's Fiction," *PMLA* 70 (1955): 632; hereafter cited in the text.

11. William Wordsworth's Preface to *The Lyrical Ballads* in *Selected Poems and Prefaces,* ed. Jack Stillinger (Boston: Houghton Mifflin, 1965), 457; hereafter cited in the text.

Wordsworth's account of the power of his own poetry in the Preface to

Notes and References

The Lyrical Ballads conveys in essence the features of Hardy's novels prior to *Jude*. "Rural life is generally chosen because in that condition, the essential passions of the heart find a better soil in which they can attain their maturity, are less under restraint, and speak a plainer and more emphatic language; because in that condition the passions of men are incorporated with the beautiful and permanent forms of nature" (Wordsworth, 447).

12. Carl J. Weber, *Hardy of Wessex: His Life and Literary Career* (New York: Columbia University Press, 1965), 205; hereafter cited in the text.

13. Lance St. John Butler, *Thomas Hardy* (Cambridge, England: Cambridge University Press, 1978), 141; hereafter cited in the text.

14. Philip M. Weinstein, " 'The Spirit Unappeased and Peregrine': Jude the Obscure," in *Thomas Hardy's Jude the Obscure*, ed. Harold Bloom (New York: Chelsea House Publishers, 1987), 133; hereafter cited in the text.

15. Ramon Saldivar, "*Jude the Obscure*: Reading and the Spirit of the Law," in Bloom, *Thomas Hardy's Jude the Obscure*, 116; hereafter cited in the text.

16. Vincent Newey, "*Jude the Obscure*: Hardy and the Forms of Making," Proceedings of the English Association North, vol. 1 (1985), 39, 42; hereafter cited in the text.

17. Norman Page, "Vision and Blindness," in Bloom, *Thomas Hardy's Jude the Obscure*, 79; hereafter cited in the text.

18. Michael Millgate, "The Tragedy of Unfulfilled Aims," in Bloom, *Thomas Hardy's Jude the Obscure*, 8; hereafter cited in the text as Millgate 1971.

19. J. I. M. Stewart, *Thomas Hardy: A Critical Biography* (London: Longman, 1971), 193; herafter cited in the text.

20. A. Alvarez, "Jude the Obscure," in *Hardy: A Collection of Critical Essays*, ed. Albert J. Guerard (Englewood Cliffs, N.J.: Prentice-Hall, 1963), 120–21; hereafter cited in the text.

21. *The Collected Letters of Thomas Hardy* (7 vols.), vol. 2, ed. Richard Purdy and Michael Millgate (Oxford: Clarendon Press, 1980), 99; hereafter *Letters* cited by volume number in the text.

22. Peter Widdowson, *Hardy in History: A Study in Literary Sociology* (London: Routledge, 1989), 74; hereafter cited in the text.

23. Patricia Ingham, Introduction to *Jude the Obscure* (Oxford: Oxford University Press, 1985), xix; hereafter cited in the text.

24. Rosemarie Morgan, *Women and Sexuality in the Novels of Thomas Hardy* (London: Routledge, 1988), 117; hereafter cited in the text.

4. A READING OF THE TEXT

1. Jorge Luis Borges, *Labyrinths* (New York: New Directions, 1964), x.

2. Arthur Mizener, *"Jude the Obscure* as a Tragedy," *Southern Review* 6 (1940–41), 408–9; hereafter cited in the text.

3. Terry Eagleton, "The Limits of Art," in Bloom, *Thomas Hardy's Jude the Obscure,* 63–64; hereafter cited in the text.

4. Quoted in A. N. Wilson, *Eminent Victorians* (London: BBC Books, 1989), 108.

5. The Nicene creed is generally accepted as the orthodox position on the question of God, Christ, and the nature of the church and is regarded by some Protestant sects as an optional confession of faith. See "Religious Creeds," in *Encyclopedia of American Religions,* 3d ed., ed. Gordon J. Melton (Detroit: Gale Research, 1989).

6. *Essays and Reviews* (London: John W. Parker & Son, West Strand, 1860), 374.

7. Marlene Springer, *Hardy's Use of Allusion* (Lawrence: University of Kansas Press, 1983), 159; hereafter cited in the text.

8. Kathleen Blake, "Sue Bridehead, 'The Woman of the Feminist Movement,' " in Bloom, *Thomas Hardy's Jude the Obscure,* 82; hereafter cited in the text.

9. Robert B. Heilman, "Hardy's Sue Bridehead," in *Hardy: The Tragic Novels,* ed. R. P. Draper (London: Macmillan, 1975), 222; hereafter cited in the text.

10. Irving Howe, *Thomas Hardy* (London: Macmillan, 1967), 142; hereafter cited in the text.

11. D. H. Lawrence, *Reflections on the Death of a Porcupine* (Bloomington: Indiana University Press, 1963), 116; hereafter cited in the text.

12. This idea was developed after the 1914 *Study* on Hardy, particularly in his work on classic American writers, and most notably in his analysis of Hester Prynne.

13. Franz Kafka, *"The Great Wall of China" and Other Pieces* (London: Martin Secker, 1933), 257.

14. John Fowles, "Hardy and the Hag," in *Thomas Hardy after Fifty Years,* ed. Lance St. John Butler (Totowa, N.J.: Rowman and Littlefield, 1977), 35; hereafter cited in the text.

15. Patricia Ingham, *Thomas Hardy* (New York: Harvester Wheatsheaf, 1989), 75; hereafter cited in the text.

16. Ian Gregor, "A Series of Seemings," in Draper, *Hardy: The Tragic Novels,* 240; hereafter cited in the text.

17. Percy Bysshe Shelley, *Prometheus Unbound,* in *John Keats and Percy Bysshe Shelley: Complete Poetical Works* (New York: Modern Library, n.d.).

18. Ronald P. Draper, "Hardy's Comic Tragedy: *Jude the Obscure,*" in *Critical Essays on Thomas Hardy,* ed. Dale Kramer (Boston: G.K. Hall & Co., 1990), 248; hereafter cited in the text.

19. Sigmund Freud, *Civilization and Its Discontents* (New York: Norton, 1961), 70; hereafter cited in the text.

20. Algernon Charles Swinburne, *Songs Before Sunrise* (London: F.S. Ellis, 1871).

21. In *Sappho: Memoir, Text, Selected Renderings and a Literal Translation,* 2d ed., trans. Henry Thornton Horton (London: David Stott, 1887).

22. John Milton, *The Doctrine and Discipline of Divorce,* vol. 3, part 2 of *The Works of John Milton,* Columbia Edition (New York: Columbia University Press, 1931).

23. *The Thoughts of the Emperor Marcus Aurelius Antoninus,* reprinted from the revised translation of George Long (London: George Bell & Sons, 1890).

24. Robert Browning, "Too Late," in *Dramatis Personae,* 2d ed. (London: J.M. Dent, 1906).

5. Conclusions

1. Quoted in J. F. C. Harrison, *Late Victorian Britain 1870–1901* (Glasgow: Fontana Press, 1990), 178; hereafter cited in the text.

2. Penny Boumelha, *Thomas Hardy and Women: Sexual Ideology and Narrative Form* (Sussex: Harvester Press, 1982); hereafter cited in the text.

3. Milan Kundera, *The Art of the Novel* (New York: Grove Press, 1986), 6; hereafter cited in the text.

4. James R. Moore, "Darwin of Down: The Evolutionist as Squarson-Naturalist," in *The Darwinian Heritage,* ed. David Kohn (Princeton, N.J.: Princeton University Press, 1985), 452; hereafter cited in the text.

5. Robert Gittings, *Thomas Hardy's Later Years* (Boston: Little, Brown & Co., 1978), 67; hereafter cited in the text.

6. Michael Steig, *Stories of Reading: Subjectivity and Literary Understanding* (Baltimore: Johns Hopkins University Press, 1989), 187–95; hereafter cited in the text.

7. Hardy began a "Shelleyan" flirtation with Florence Henniker while *Jude the Obscure* was in incubation. Mrs. Henniker, the immediate inspiration for Sue, was a sophisticated and beautiful woman, a society lady with three

published novels to her credit. She kept Hardy at arm's length, and his equivocal desire for her probably colored the tragic love story of Jude and Sue. Sue-Florence Henniker provides Jude-Hardy with both the attraction of incest and the fantasy of permanent chasteness. "Shelleyan" is a euphemism in Hardy for Oedipal, or incest, fantasy.

Steig claims that Jude and Sue roughly enact the conditions of an unresolved Oedipus complex described in the first two of Freud's *Contributions to the Psychology of Love*, "A Special Type of Choice of Object Made by Men," and "On the Universal Tendency to Debasement in the Sphere of Love." These conditions are those of "the man who needs to be jealous before he can feel truly passionate towards a woman," and who "repeatedly reenacts the scene of love for the mother and jealousy of the father, with a concomitant phantasy of rescuing the woman (mother)," and "the tendency to be impotent with one's wife but not with a 'loose woman' or a prostitute" because "the 'purity' of the wife (who is unconsciously seen as a mother) makes her a taboo sexual object" (see Steig, 193–95).

8. Schopenhauer seems to evoke *Jude* strikingly in the following passage:

> The life of every individual, viewed as a whole and in general, and when only its most significant features are emphasized, is really a tragedy; but gone through in detail it has the character of a comedy. For the doings and worries of the day, week, the mishaps of every hour, are all brought about by chance that is always bent on some mischievous trick; they are nothing but scenes from a comedy. The never-fulfilled wishes, the frustrated efforts, the hopes mercilessly blighted by fate, the unfortunate mistakes of the whole life, with increasing suffering and death at the end, always give us a tragedy. Thus, as if fate wished to add mockery to the misery of our existence, our life must contain all the woes of tragedy, and yet we cannot even assert the dignity of tragic characters, but, in the broad detail of life, are inevitably the foolish characters of a comedy. (*The World as Will and Representation*, vol. 1, trans. E. F. J. Payne [New York: Dover Publications, 1966], 322)

9. From Yeats's essay "The Tragic Theatre" in *The Cutting of An Agate* (London, 1910); reprinted in *Essays and Introductions* (London, 1961), 240–45.

10. See, for instance, the opening chapter in Richard Sewall's *The Vision of Tragedy* (New Haven: Yale University Press, 1980); the essays by Murray Krieger and Arthur Miller in Robert Corrigan's *Tragedy: Vision and Form* (San Francisco: Chandler Publishing Co., 1965); and R. P. Draper's *Tragedy: Developments in Criticism* (Hong Kong: Macmillan, 1980).

Annotated Bibliography

Primary Sources

The Collected Letters of Thomas Hardy. 7 vols. Edited by Richard Purdy and Michael Millgate. Oxford: Clarendon Press, 1978–1988. The definitive edition of the letters.

Collected Poems of Thomas Hardy. New York: Macmillan, 1937.

Jude the Obscure: An Authoritative Text, Backgrounds and Sources, Criticism. Edited by Norman Page. New York: Norton, 1978.

The Life and Work of Thomas Hardy. Edited by Michael Millgate. London: Macmillan, 1984. Revised edition of Florence Hardy's *Early Life* and *Later Years,* originally published under Hardy's second wife's name, but written mostly by Hardy himself. A strange book in which Hardy, with the help of his wife, assembled personal impressions, anecdotes, portions of letters, and notes on social engagements, travel, and art—his "ghosted autobiography." Millgate restores many of the excisions made after Hardy's death: for example, references to his first wife and aristocrats he met, and disgusted reactions to negative reviews of his work.

The Mayor of Casterbridge: An Authoritative Text, Backgrounds, Criticism. Edited by James K. Robinson. New York: Norton, 1977.

The Return of the Native: An Authoritative Text, Background, Criticism. Edited by James Gindin. New York: Norton, 1969.

Tess of the d'Urbervilles: An Authoritative Text, Hardy and the Novel, Criticism. 2d ed. Edited by Scott Elledge. New York: Norton, 1979. First published in 1965.

Thomas Hardy's Personal Writings: Prefaces, Literary Opinions, Reminiscences. Edited by Harold Orel. Lawrence: University of Kansas Press, 1966. A collection of Hardy's occasional nonfiction writings, containing four important essays—"The Dorsetshire Labourer," "The Profitable Reading of Fiction," "Candour in English Fiction," and "The Science of Fiction"—as well as Hardy's prefaces to his own novels.

Secondary Sources

Book-length Studies

Allen, Walter. *The English Novel: A Short Critical History.* New York: E. P. Dutton, 1957.

Bloom, Harold. *Thomas Hardy's Jude the Obscure.* New York: Chelsea House Publishers, 1987. This outstanding collection includes essays by Gregor, Eagleton, Blake, Saldivar, and Weinstein.

Boumelha, Penny. *Thomas Hardy and Women: Sexual Ideology and Narrative Form.* Sussex: Harvester Press, 1982. A brilliant combination of Marxist and feminist analysis.

Butler, Lance St. John. *Thomas Hardy.* Cambridge, England: Cambridge University Press, 1978. An excellent general study of the major novels, discussing *Jude* as an allegory, a sociological novel, and a psychological novel.

———, ed. *Thomas Hardy After Fifty Years.* Totowa, N.J.: Rowman and Littlefield, 1977. Contains an excellent essay by John Fowles.

Cecil, David. *Hardy the Novelist: An Essay in Criticism.* London: Constable & Co., 1943. An essay in the grand style, at one time a major introduction to Hardy's fiction. Cecil describes the influences shaping Hardy, his affinities, and his unique gifts and shortcomings.

Corrigan, Robert W., ed. *Tragedy: Vision and Form.* San Francisco: Chandler Publishing Co., 1965.

Cox, R. G., ed. *Thomas Hardy: The Critical Heritage.* New York: Barnes & Noble, 1970. An anthology of more than 75 contemporary reviews of Hardy's novels and volumes of poetry.

Draper, R. P., ed. *Hardy: The Tragic Novels.* London: Macmillan, 1975. Some excellent essays, including Heilman's and Gregor's on *Jude.*

———. *Tragedy: Development in Criticism.* Hong Kong: Macmillan, 1980.

Draper, R. P. and Martin S. Ray, eds. *An Annotated Critical Bibliography of Thomas Hardy.* Ann Arbor: University of Michigan Press, 1989. An indispensable reference.

Essays and Reviews. London: John W. Parker & Son, West Strand, 1860.

Forster, E. M. *Aspects of the Novel.* New York: Harcourt Brace & World, 1954. First published in 1927. Faults Hardy for imposing plot upon character rather than making plot reveal hidden psychology.

Gittings, Robert. *Thomas Hardy's Later Years.* Boston: Little, Brown & Co., 1978.

———. *Young Thomas Hardy.* Boston: Little, Brown & Co., 1975. Volume I of Gittings's "challenging, exciting, iconoclastic biography" (Draper). Gittings is one of the two chief Hardy biographers.

Annotated Bibliography

Guerard, Albert J., ed. *Hardy: A Collection of Critical Essays.* Englewood Cliffs, N.J.: Prentice-Hall, 1963. Contains A. Alvarez's important essay on *Jude.*

Howe, Irving. *Thomas Hardy.* London: Macmillan, 1967. A beautifully written general study.

Ingham, Patricia. *Thomas Hardy.* New York: Harvester Wheatsheaf, 1989. A brilliant feminist study.

Kramer, Dale, ed. *Critical Essays on Thomas Hardy: The Novels.* Boston: G. K. Hall & Co., 1990. Kramer's introduction provides a good general discussion of the milestones and developments in Hardy criticism.

Lawrence, D. H. *Reflections on the Death of a Porcupine.* Bloomington, Ind.: Indiana University Press, 1963. First published 1925.

————. *Phoenix: the Posthumous Papers of D. H. Lawrence.* Edited and with an Introduction by Edward D. McDonald. New York: The Viking Press, 1972. First published 1936. Contains "Study of Thomas Hardy." Chapters 3, 4, and 9 of this classic are indispensable reading for students of *Jude.*

Millgate, Michael. *Thomas Hardy: A Biography.* New York: Random House, 1982. A balanced, thorough work of scholarship.

Morgan, Rosemarie. *Women and Sexuality in the Novels of Thomas Hardy.* London: Routledge, 1988. Sees the tragedy of *Jude* as deriving from Sue's failure to live as a sexual being.

Rutland, William R. *Thomas Hardy: A Study of His Writings and Their Background.* New York: Russell & Russell, 1962. First published in 1938. Excellent introductory chapters on Hardy's intellectual development and the cultural influences shaping his works.

Sewall, Richard B. *The Vision of Tragedy.* New Haven: Yale University Press, 1980.

Springer, Marlene. *Hardy's Use of Allusion.* Lawrence: University of Kansas Press, 1983. Offers an illuminating study of Hardy's use of allusion in *Jude.*

Steig, Michael. *Stories of Reading: Subjectivity and Literary Understanding.* Baltimore: Johns Hopkins University Press, 1989. Contains a brilliant psychoanalytic interpretation of *Jude* in a discussion of the novel as a parody of Shelley's "The Revolt of Islam."

Stewart, J. I. M. *Thomas Hardy: A Critical Biography.* London: Longman, 1971. A level-headed, truculent, occasionally witty general study.

Weber, Carl J. *Hardy of Wessex: His Life and Literary Career.* New York: Columbia University Press, 1965. Originally published in 1940. Compares *Jude* to *King Lear.*

Widdowson, Peter. *Hardy in History: A Study in Literary Sociology.* London: Routledge, 1989. A powerful and provocative view of Hardy as a political writer.

Woolf, Virginia. *The Common Reader: Second Series*. London: Hogarth Press, 1932. An appreciative general assessment.

Essays and Articles

Alvarez, A. "Jude the Obscure." In *Hardy: A Collection of Critical Essays*, edited by Albert J. Guerard, 113–22. Englewood Cliffs, N.J.: Prentice-Hall, 1963. Originally published in *Jude the Obscure*. New York: New American Library, 1961. Sue and Arabella are seen as embodiments of something inside Jude himself, and Jude in turn is an embodiment "of the loneliness, deprivation, and regret" that is the constant theme of Hardy's best poetry. In Alvarez's view, not thwarted ambition or marriage but Jude's loneliness is the central subject of the novel.

Bartlett, Phyllis. " 'Seraph of Heaven': A Shelleyan Dream in Hardy's Fiction." *PMLA* 70 (1955): 624–35.

Blake, Kathleen. "Sue Bridehead, 'The Woman of the Feminist Movement.' " In *Thomas Hardy's Jude the Obscure*, edited by Harold Bloom, 81–102. New York: Chelsea House Publishers, 1987. Originally published in *Studies in English Literature 1500–1900* 18, no. 4 (Autumn 1978). A highly plausible and stimulating feminist reading of Sue, whose relationships with men are explained as experiments in self-emancipation.

Brown, Douglas. "A Novel of Character and Environment." In *Hardy: the Tragic Novels*, edited by R. P. Draper, 158–64. London: Macmillan, 1975. Originally published in *Thomas Hardy*. London: E. Arnold, 1954. Sees Tess as an allegory for "the agricultural community in its moment of ruin."

Draper, Ronald P. "Hardy's Comic Tragedy: *Jude the Obscure*." In *Critical Essays on Thomas Hardy: The Novels*, edited by Dale Kramer, 243–54. Boston: G. K. Hall & Co., 1990. An excellent analysis of the tragic-comic elements in the novel.

Eagleton, Terry. "The Limits of Art." In *Thomas Hardy's Jude the Obscure*, edited by Harold Bloom, 61–71. New York: Chelsea House Publishers, 1987. Originally published in *Jude the Obscure*, edited by Terry Eagleton, 1974. Reads *Jude* as Hardy's "most masterly exploration of the limits of liberation in Victorian society."

Fowles, John. "Hardy and the Hag." In *Thomas Hardy After Fifty Years*, edited by Lance St. John Butler, 28–42. Totowa, N.J.: Rowman and Littlefield, 1977. A Freudian analysis, sparkling and witty. Confirms my idea that *Jude* discloses an intimately shameful fantasy.

Gregor, Ian. "A Series of Seemings." In *Hardy: The Tragic Novels*, edited by R. P. Draper, 227–47. London: Macmillan, 1975. Originally published in *The Great Web*, 1974. Argues that Jude's and Sue's attempts to live unconventional lives are doomed to collapse owing to the pressures of society.

Annotated Bibliography

Heilman, Robert B. "Hardy's Sue Bridehead." In *Hardy: The Tragic Novels*, edited by R. P. Draper, 209–26. London: Macmillan, 1975. Originally published in *Nineteenth-Century Fiction* 20, 1965. An interesting psychological reading of Sue as a case study more than an example of failed liberation.

Ingham, Patricia. Introduction to *Jude the Obscure*. Oxford: Oxford University Press, 1985. Reads the novel as "the most powerful indictment of the sexual and class oppression of its time." A brilliant essay written with tight, muscular prose.

Jowett, Benjamin. "On the Interpretation of Scripture." In *Essays and Reviews*, 330–433. London: John W. Parker & Son, 1860.

Millgate, Michael. "The Tragedy of Unfulfilled Aims." In *Thomas Hardy's Jude the Obscure*, edited by Harold Bloom, 7–17. New York: Chelsea House Publishers, 1987. Originally entitled "Jude the Obscure" and published in *Thomas Hardy: His Career as a Novelist*. New York: Random House, 1971. Sees *Jude* as modelled on *Oedipus Rex* in its highly self-conscious patterning.

Mizener, Arthur. "*Jude the Obscure* as a Tragedy." *Southern Review* 6 (1940–41): 203–13; also appears in *Jude the Obscure*, edited by Norman Page, 406–14. New York: Norton.

Newey, Vincent. "*Jude the Obscure*: Hardy and the Forms of Making." Proceedings of the English Association North, v.i., 1985: 29–51. Offers an eloquent explanation of the ironically conflicting perspectives in *Jude*.

Page, Norman. "Vision and Blindness." In *Thomas Hardy's Jude the Obscure*, edited by Harold Bloom, 73–80. New York: Chelsea House Publishers, 1987. Originally published in *Thomas Hardy*, 1977.

Saldivar, Ramon. "*Jude the Obscure*: Reading and the Spirit of the Law." In *Thomas Hardy's Jude the Obscure*, edited by Harold Bloom, 103–18. New York: Chelsea House Publishers, 1987. Originally published in *ELH* 50, no. 3 (1983). Argues that a delineation of a consistent point of view in *Jude* is impossible, that the novel is "an allegory of the breakdown of the referential system," and that it is about reversals and failure.

Weinstein, Philip M. " 'The Spirit Unappeased and Peregrine': Jude the Obscure." In *Thomas Hardy's Jude the Obscure*, edited by Harold Bloom, 119–35. New York: Chelsea House Publishers, 1987. Originally published in *The Semantics of Desire: Changing Models of Identity from Dickens to Joyce*, 1984. A brilliant, influential piece. Weinstein argues that Jude conspires in his own downfall.

Background Reading

Anderson, C. A. *School and Society in England*. Annals of American Research. Public Affairs Press, 1952.

Annan, Noel. *Leslie Stephen: A Godless Victorian*. 1st American ed. New York: Random House, 1984. An excellent cultural history.

Arnstein, Walter L. *Britain Yesterday and Today, 1830 to the Present*. 2d ed. Lexington, Mass.: D. C. Heath and Co., 1971. First published in 1966.

Bloom, Harold. *Thomas Hardy*. New York: Chelsea House Publishers, 1987.

Butler, Josephine E., ed. *Woman's Work and Woman's Culture*. London: Macmillan, 1869.

Cohen, I. Bernard. "Three Notes on the Reception of Darwin's Ideas on Natural Selection (Henry Baker Tristram, Alfred Newton, Samuel Wilberforce)." In *The Darwinian Heritage*, edited by David Kohn, 589–607. Princeton, N.J.: Princeton University Press, 1985.

Eliot, T. S. *After Strange Gods*. New York: Harcourt Brace Jovanovich, 1934.

Fussell, Paul. *The Great War and Modern Memory*. New York: Oxford University Press, 1975.

Garwood, Helen. *Thomas Hardy: An Illustration of the Philosophy of Schopenhauer*. Folcroft, Pa.: Folcroft Press, 1969. Originally published in 1911.

Giordano, Frank R. *"I'd Have My Life Unbe": Thomas Hardy's Self-Destructive Characters*. University: University of Alabama Press, 1984.

Goode, John. *Thomas Hardy: The Offensive Truth*. Oxford: Basil Blackwell, 1988.

Gordon, David J. *D. H. Lawrence as Literary Critic*. New Haven: Yale University Press, 1966.

Harrison, J. F. C. *Late Victorian Britain 1870–1901*. Glasgow: Fontana Press, 1990. An excellent cultural history.

Kohn, David, ed. *The Darwinian Heritage*. Princeton, N.J.: Princeton University Press, 1985.

Kundera, Milan. *The Art of the Novel*. New York: Grove Press, 1986.

Llosa, Mario Vargas. *The Perpectual Orgy: Flaubert and Madame Bovary*. Translated from the Spanish by Helen Lane. New York: Farrar, Straus Giroux, 1986.

Marriott, Stuart. *Backstairs to a Degree: Demands for an Open University in Late Victorian England*. Leeds: J. Jackman and Company, 1981.

Mill, John Stuart. *On Liberty: Annotated Text, Sources and Background, Criticism*. Edited by David Spitz. New York: Norton, 1975.

Moore, James R. "Darwin of Down: The Evolutionist as Squarson-Naturalist." In *The Darwinian Heritage*, edited by David Kohn, 435–81. Princeton, N.J.: Princeton University Press, 1985.

Rubinstein, David. *Before the Suffragettes: Women's Emancipation in the 1890's*. New York: St. Martin's Press, 1986.

Annotated Bibliography

Sanderson, Michael, ed. *The Universities in the Nineteenth Century*. London: Routledge & Kegan Paul, 1975.

Schiller, Gertrud. *Iconography of Christian Art*. Translated by Janet Seligman. Greenwich, Conn.: New York Graphic Society, 1971. Originally published in German in 1966.

Schopenhauer, Arthur. *The World as Will and Representation*. Translated by E. F. J. Payne. New York: Dover Publications, 1966.

Steinberg, Leo. *The Sexuality of Christ in Renaissance Art and in Modern Oblivion*. New York: Pantheon Books, 1983.

Sumner, Rosemary. *Thomas Hardy: Psychological Novelist*. New York: St. Martin's Press, 1981.

Tillyard, A. I. *A History of University Reform: From 1800 A.D. to the Present Time*. Cambridge, England: W. Heffer and Sons, 1913.

Vicinus, Martha, ed. *Suffer and Be Still: Women in the Victorian Age*. Bloomington: Indiana University Press, 1972.

Wilson, A. N. *Eminent Victorians*. London: BBC Books, 1989.

Index

Index

Eggs, symbolism of, 99–100
Eliot, George, 115
Ellis, Havelock: *Man and Woman*, 89; review of *Jude*, 15
Epigraphs, 82–87; Part First, 83; Part Second, 84; Part Third, 84–85; Part Fourth, 85; Part Fifth, 85–86; Part Sixth, 86–87
"Epipsychidion" (Shelley), 17, 31, 62
Essays and Reviews, 4–5
Esther, book of, 86–87
Evolution, 88–89. *See also* Darwin's theory; Natural selection theory

Far from the Madding Crowd (Hardy), 22
Fatalism, in *Jude*, 101
Father Time. *See* Little Father Time
Fawcett, Millicent Garrett, 24
Fawcett Society, 24, 93
Fawley, Jude, 4
Fawley curse, 67, 106
Female sexuality, 6
Flaubert, 107
Forster, E. M., 16
Fowles, John: on artistic process, 62, 110; on *Jude*, 113–14

García-Marquez, Gabriel, 114
Gifford, Emma, 8
Gittings, Robert, 22, 109
Gosse, Edmund, 21, 57, 106; review of *Jude*, 14–15; on Sue, 23–24
Gregor, Ian: on Hardy, 78; on Jude, 68, 72
Group of Noble Dames, A (Hardy), 13

Hardy, Emma, 105, 106, 107
Hardy, Jemina, 22, 107, 109

Hardy, Thomas, *103–7*; attitudes toward faith and class, 94; austerity in male characters of, 40; autobiography of, 45; causality in novels of, 16–17; on charges of pessimism, 18; childhood of, 7–8; on construction of *Jude*, 57; D. H. Lawrence on, 17; dreams of becoming clergyman, 104–5; early criticism of, 13–16; on evolution, 5–6; *Far from the Madding Crowd*, 22; on female suffrage, 92–93; on form of *Jude*, 21–22; "ghosted" autobiography of, 22; Horace Moule and, 9; interest in "new woman," 78; lower-class origins of, 22–23; marriage to Emma Gifford, 8–9, 105–7; mother of, 7–8, 22; *The Mayor of Casterbridge*, 17, 112; multiple points of view of, 43–44; Oedipal fantasy of, 110; pessimism of, 6, 11, 23, 44; point of view in novels of, 18–20; prejudice against flesh, 61; preparation for career in Church, 3, 4; *The Pursuit of the Well-Beloved*, 108; rationalism of heroes in his novels, 5–6; reputation as novelist, 12; *The Return of the Native*, 18, 40, 112; sexual development of, 8; sexual impotence of, 9; Shelley's influence on, 18; suicidal wish of, 9; *Tess of the d'Urbervilles*, 13, 14, 18, 40, 112
"Hearts Insurgent" (Hardy), 13
Heilman, Robert, 51
Henniker, Florence, 93, 108
Hope, as theme, 70
Howe, Irving, 51

132

Index

Huxley, Thomas Henry, 102; in defense of Darwin's theory, 5

Ibsen, plays of, 6
Infant death rates, 89
Ingham, Patricia: on ambiguity in *Jude*, 43; on Hardy's treatment of women, 63–64, 88, 92; on Sue, 63
"In Tenebris" (Hardy), 13, 32
Ireland, independence of, 6

Jowett, Benjamin, 5, 48
Jude: alienation from Sue, 74; Arabella and, 37–39, 56–57; blindness of, 20; character of, 35; childhood of, 35; on children, 79–80; compatible neuroses of Sue and, 67; consummation of love between Sue and, 66–67; death of, 79, 81–82; happiness of Sue and, 67–69; Hardy's changing perspective on, 94–98; Horace Moule as model for, 9; impatience with faith, 58; loss of faith, 69–70; meaning of name, 32; on parenthood, 93; reader's sympathy for, 32–33; second marriage to Arabella, 78–79; subjugation of Sue by, 25; on Sue, 80–81; Sue and, 58–60; youth of, 36–37
Jude the Obscure, 10–12; as allegory of repression of erotic impulses, 110–11; allusions to Jesus in, 33–34, 82; ambiguity in, 19–20, 29–31, 43–44, 102; Christminster in, 33–34; criticism of, 14–15; cultural prejudices of time and, 31; early forms of, 13; epigraphs, 29, 82–87; fatalism in, 101; feminist reading of, 23–25;

form of, 20–22; Hardy on form of, 21–22; idea for, 13; importance of, 10–12; marriage and women's social position in, 7; Marxist reading of, 22–23; Part First "At Marygreen," 33–41; Part Second "At Christminster," 41–48; Part Third "At Melchester," 48–58; Part Fourth "At Shaston," 58–64; Part Fifth "At Aldbrickham and Elsewhere," 64–71; Part Sixth "At Christminster Again," 71–82; pessimism in, 16–18, 110–11; pig sticking in, 38–40; as psychic drama about deadlock, 113; reputation as novel, 12; shame in, 32; subject of, 10–12; symmetrical construction of, 99

Kafka, 58
Karenina, Anna, 94
Keble: *The Christian Year*, 3
Kundera, Milan: on ambiguity in *Jude*, 114; *The Art of the Novel*, 29; on birth of novel, 94; on Hardy's juggling point of view, 98

Lawrence, D. H., 15–16, 17; on Christianity, 54; on Father Time, 75; on Hardy, 111–12; on Jude and Sue, 40, 61, 77; on pig sticking, 40; *Sons and Lovers*, 109, 112; *Study of Thomas Hardy*, 54, 112–13; on Sue, 54–55, 56, 111
Life (Hardy), 45
Life's Little Ironies (Hardy), 13
Linton, Eliza Lynn, 103

Index

Little Father Time, 6, 15, 66, 68,
  69, 74, 91, 93; adoption of,
  79–80; description of, 98; as
  ego, 75; as Jude's inner reality,
  79
Long, George, 85

Macbeth (Shakespeare), 39
Man and Woman (Ellis), 89
Marriage: institution of, 93;
  unhappiness in, 10; women's
  role in, 6
Max Gate, 8, 22, 106, 107
Mayor of Casterbridge, The
  (Hardy), 17, 112
Meditations (Marcus Aurelius
  Antoninus), 85–86
Metamorphoses (Ovid), 84
Mill, John Stuart, 60; influence on
  Hardy, 5; On Liberty, 5; The
  Subjection of Women, 90
Millgate, Michael, 5, 8, 9, 14, 20,
  32, 57, 106
Milton, John, 38, 54; The Doctrine
  and Discipline of Divorce, 85;
  Paradise Lost, 76
Missal for the Use of the Laity, The
  (Hardy), 5
Mizener, Arthur, 39
Morgan, Rosemarie, 24–25
Motherhood, limitations of, 91–92
Moule, Horace, 9, 105

Names, Hardy's play on words and,
  101
Natural selection theory, 102–3;
  definition, 102
Newey, Vincent, 20
Novel, birth of, 94

Oedipus (Sophocles), 20
Oliphant, Mrs., 14, 15
On the Origin of Species (Darwin),
  4, 88

O'Shea, Captain, 6
Ovid: Metamorphoses, 84
Oxbridge, 104–5
Oxford University: in medieval
  times, 3–4; women at, 7

Page, Norman: on form of Jude,
  20; on Hardy's shifting point
  of view, 44
Paradise Lost (Milton), 76
Parenthood, 93
Parnell, Charles Stuart, 6
Phillotson, 57, 60–61, 77–78; as
  Hardy's superego, 108; letting
  Sue leave, 97–98; on marriage,
  93; piano of, 100–101; Sue
  and, 60
Pigs, symbolism of, 100
Pilgrim's Progress, 34
Prometheus Unbound (Shelley), 70
Prostitution: crusade against, 90; in
  mid-Victorian England, 7
Pursuit of the Well-Beloved, The
  (Hardy), 108

Queen's College, 7

Rainbow, The (Lawrence), 16, 112
Renaissance, sexuality in, 54
Return of the Native, The (Hardy),
  18, 112; Clym Yeobright in, 40
"Revolt of Islam, The" (Shelley),
  17, 92, 113–14
Rushdie, Salman, 114
Rutland, William, 17, 18

Saldivar, Ramon, 48; on Hardy's
  point of view, 19
Sappho, 84–85
Schopenhauer, 18, 114; on tragedy,
  81
Sexual differences, evolution and,
  89

Index

Shame, 93–101; introduction, 93–94; undercutting Jude, 94–101

Shelley, Percy, 31; "Epipsychidion," 17, 31, 62; influence on Hardy, 17; *Prometheus Unbound*, 70; "The Revolt of Islam," 92, 113–14

"Simpletons, The" (Hardy), 13; as title, 44, 58

Songs Before Sunrise (Swinburne), 84

Sons and Lovers (Lawrence), 109, 112

Sophocles: *Oedipus*, 20

Sparks, Maria, 109

Sparks, Martha, 8, 109, 110

Sparks, Rebecca, 8, 109–10

Sparks, Tryphena, 8, 110

Spencer, Herbert: on abstract thinking in women, 89; on misogyny, 63; *The Study of Sociology*, 63, 88

Springer, Marlene, 50, 56

Steig, Michael, 113–14

Stephen, Leslie, 22; *An Agnostic's Apology*, 103

Stewart, J.I.M., 21; on Arabella, 40; on Fawley curse, 67

Study of Sociology, The (Spencer), 63, 88

Study of Thomas Hardy (Lawrence), 15–16, 54, 112–13

Subjection of Women, The (Mill), 90

Sue Bridehead, 11–12; antipathy to motherhood, 75; attacks on Christianity, 53; case for feminist reading of, 88–93; character of, 50–55; compatible neuroses of Jude and, 67; consummation of love between Jude and, 66–67; death of her children, 74; D. H. Lawrence on, 54–55; feminist reading of, 23–25, 88–93; happiness of Jude and, 67–69; jealousy of, 64–66; Jude and, 58–60; Jude on, 80–81; Jude's alienation from, 74; models for, 8; Phillotson and, 47, 55, 60; religious feelings of, 75–76, 78, 80; role as substitute for Christminster in Jude's life, 42–43, 44–45; sexual repression of, 50, 52–53, 58–62, 64–65, 91–92; as substitute for Christminster, 49–50

Suffragist movement, 24

Swinburne: *Songs Before Sunrise*, 84

Taylor, Tinker, 72

Tess of the d'Urbervilles (Hardy), 13, 18, 112; Angel Clare in, 40; reviews of, 14

Tetuphenary, T., in *Jude*, 47

"Too Late" (Browning), 87

Transcendent love, in *Jude*, 31

Tyndall, John, 5

Vilbert, in *Jude*, 35–36, 64, 68, 69, 81–82

Ward, Mrs. Humphry, 103

Weber, Carl, 19

Weinstein, Philip, 48; on Hardy's point of view toward Jude, 43; on Jude, 19, 41, 43; on Jude and Sue, 54; on Jude's idealism, 72; on Jude's second marriage to Arabella, 79

Well-Beloved, The (Hardy), 13, 110

"Wessex Heights" (Hardy), 13, 32

Wharton, H. T., 85

Index

Widdowson, Peter, 107; on Hardy's
    pessimism, 44; on Jude as
    Marxist novel, 22–23
Wilberforce, Samuel, 5, 102–3
"Wise passiveness," 115
Woman Who Did, The (Allen), 90
Women: childbearing and, 89–90;
    education and, 7; employment
    and, 7, 90; evolution and
    sexual differences between men
    and, 89; Hardy on vote of, 24;
    limitations of motherhood and,
    91–92; menstruation and

deceit in, 89; oppression of, 6,
    92; participation in politics by,
    91; right to vote, 7, 24; role in
    marriage, 6; Spencer on
    abstract thinking in, 89
Woolf, Virginia, 16–17
Workingman, oppression of, 92
World as Will and Idea, The
    (Hardy), 18

Yeats, 115

Zorobabel, 83

The Author

Gary Adelman teaches English at the University of Illinois in Urbana-Champaign. He has written a novel, a book on D. H. Lawrence, and has authored Twayne studies on *Heart of Darkness* and *Anna Karenina*.